Being Me:
A GUIDE TO BRANDING MYSELF EVERYDAY

By: Amira Shiraz

Paperback edition first published by
Amira Shiraz, Inc. in 2011
●

Amira Shiraz, Inc.
525 South 4th Street
Suite 585
Philadelphia, PA 19147
USA
●

Tel: 215-600-1603
Fax: 215-600-1613
www.AmiraShiraz.com

Special discounts on B.ME books are available
to
corporations, schools, associations and other
organizations.

For details, please contact us.
www.BrandingMyselfEveryday.com

Book design by Holly Staub.

Printed in the United States of America.
ISBN-13: 978-0615502472
ISBN-10: 0615502474
LCCN: 2011932369

TO EVERYONE THAT'S A DREAMER
AND THOSE THAT BELIEVE IN GREATNESS.

CONTENTS:

Authors Note

Acknowledgments

Creating B.ME! certainly has been a process. The book you are about to read started as a thought to help others achieve their goals and better their way of life. At its essence and core, I'm proud to say that it still is just that. Easy to grasp concepts that young professionals and people at the beginning and transitional stages of their life would be able to find value and guidance as they continue on their journey to where we all hope to arrive-**SUCCESS**.

To achieve great things you need great people. B.ME!'s success is just as much yours as it is my own. It was created for you; an individual seeking knowledge, input and assistance on the path of personal building. As you read the content within and follow through the exercises, know that the greatest accomplishment that this book could be given, far greater than any review or accolade is this: knowing that it helped you achieve at least one of the goals you've identified for yourself.

These parts wouldn't be created if it were not for people that walked along the path of my life and my own personal brand building. To Rakeem Christmas, like most things, this thought started with you in mind and it was because of you I was able to continue. There was no greater case study that I could have been blessed with than you. On the down days, of writer's block and needing an extra push that this project would see a sweet ending, Evelyn Hamid, was my backbone. There is something beyond special about a mother's love that gives you strength you weren't even sure you had. Having you by my side daily, was the greatest support system I could have asked for. Ryan Joseph, our journey together for twelve years has given me more knowledge and taught me how important trust in oneself really is.

I've lived my life (or least I try to) without fear and trusting that my internal compass leads me to the opportunities and people to support seeing my goals through.

Acknowledgments

Shawn Smith trusted me, blindly, in creating Amira Shiraz, Inc (ASI). I wouldn't have had the opportunities without a business partner like you.

Elizabeth Trubey started off as an intern with me and blossomed into a professional during her time with ASI. Of all my support staff, you understood the goal and treated the project as your own. I wouldn't have gotten to the end without you.

I've worked with many graphic designers but none quite like Holly Staub. Our final product truly exceeded my expectations.

For all my clients, both past and present, I owe the greatest appreciation to you for entrusting me with building your personal brands. For every strategic plan created and every branding pitch, it provided me with real life anecdotes to channel to help others. Allowing me to help you navigate your individual gifts and talents provided me with the confidence that I could help others achieve their own.

While there are so many people that I owe a personal Thank You to, I couldn't have asked for a better sounding board than in Rob Brown, Robert Murphy, Nasha Rivera, D'Andre Archie, Ilalee Harrison, Rico Joseph and Kevin Givens. Individually and collectively you've all touched my life in such a way that I was able to use your positivity and support to guide me and see this project through.

In a day and age of war and country collisions, I've found a new appreciation and respect for all the men and women who serve our country in the military. To all of you, I Thank You for allowing us to enjoy the freedoms that we all take for granted each day. Sobers Joseph and Bernard Blackburn, Thank You.

Introduction

What would you like to be known for? Are you the philanthropist who's focused and committed to raising awareness about a certain illness? Or do you fantasize and see yourself as a superstar attending red carpet events? Maybe you are somewhere in between and hoping to be a big fish in a little pond with your talents. There is a good chance that you are not sure what you want your mark to be in this world and for those blessed to be multi-talented it is not easy to decipher which ones to focus on.

This guide to personal branding teaches you why these skills are important everyday of your life. From your personal to your professional life, your brand flows through both sides. If you have not sat down and strategized how you plan on making your brand work for you, there is a very good chance that you are losing opportunities to others who have. As our world becomes more about who is the strongest, fastest and smartest, how do you fold within the margins of what we equate to being a success?

Creating a brand is not done overnight. It takes time, care and effort. As you grow in your life and experience new things, so does your brand. After all, it is a reflection of you. Strong personal brands are not crafted by managers or someone behind the scenes pulling strings. The ones that last and are memorable are those who were molded by the individuals themselves, whose name they bear- YOU!

The brand called YOU is special. It is unique and not quite like any other. The sooner you realize that, the quicker you will grasp the concepts and directions contained in the chapters ahead. Do not sell yourself short. Just because you are not a mainstream public figure does not mean you cannot use the very same tactics and learn the skills, taught to them, to reach your own personal pinnacles of success.

Even without a publicist, personal PR can be easy without being overbearing. Know your strengths. Play off of them. Accept your weaknesses. Work on them.

Be clear about what you want to achieve. It makes it easier to know once you have arrived there. You are already ahead of the curve for taking the first step in learning how to create your personal brand. It is up to you to see it through.

Let us re-evaluate your personal marketing plan and help you create one if you have not completed one. In personal or professional marketing the bases are the same. The strategies of a Fortune 500 company does not differ much from a solidified artist on the billboard charts. Learning these tricks of the trade now will make sure you land that dream internship or job, materialize a hobby into a venture and change the perception of you to increase your net-worth in your network. The current world we live in always rewards those with an edge. Have you identified yours?

Be clear about what you want to achieve. It makes it easier to know once you have arrived there.

Part 1:

Defining and Creating Your Personal Brand

"**Personal branding** is about managing your name — even if you don't own a business — in a world of misinformation, disinformation, and semi-permanent Google records. Going on a date? Chances are that your "blind" date has Googled your name. Going to a job interview? Ditto."

-Tim Ferriss,
Author of the *4-Hour Work Week*

Chapter 1

What Is a Personal Brand?

"As a brand, you are your own free agent: you have the freedom to create the career path that links your talents and interests to the right position or path."

-Dan Schawbel, Personal Branding expert and author of Me 2.0

What you'll learn in this chapter:

- Definition of a personal brand
- Importance of personal branding
- Branding in all industries
- Components of a personal brand
- Perception = Reality

13

News flash:

You have been branded. Although most people are unaware of it, this has happened to everyone. We all have a reputation or a personal image by which other people recognize us, whether we have put conscious effort into constructing this image or not. For the most part, it is what people have heard, read about, or are able to see physically that gives them a go-to mental image of us: clothing, physical characteristics, actions, rumors and blog entries. Although this mental image may have some relevance, it is not a true personal brand. It has been constructed by other people. Do not you want your personal brand to be, well...personal?

Simply stated: "Define your brand, or your brand will define you."

What Exactly Do You Mean By Personal Brand?

Your personal brand is "the powerful, clear, positive idea that comes to mind when people think of you." It comes from your vision of where you want to go, what you want to accomplish, and what you want to be recognized for. Personal branding is the process of taking your skills, personality and unique characteristics and packaging them into a powerful identity that sets you apart from the crowd.

It makes you recognizable.
Relatable.
Powerful.

If you thought only products have brands, you thought wrong.

Jordan Brand, Verizon Wireless, Fruit of the Loom, Penn State University, Gatorade, UPS, Oprah, McDonald's, Target.

Unless you have been living under a rock for the past decade, you will easily recognize these names. But will you recognize these **names as brands**? The truth is, virtually everything can be branded. Branding- whether it be company, product, or personal- is a form of marketing. It is simply sales. Just as a company markets their brand to sell products or services, people market their brand to sell themselves. A brand is the collection of skills, characteristics, slogans, and logos used to entice the target audience into believing in them, trusting in them and, ultimately investing in them. A successful brand creates an immediate idea in your mind.

Nike scatters stores, magazines, commercials and billboards with pictures of athletes pulling off the perfect dunk, or completing a gravity-defying goal shot, splashes the swoosh on it, and urges you to "Just Do It". Burger King places a crown on your head to make you feel like, well...a king, and reminds you that you can "Have It Your Way". Apple encourages you to "Think Different" while flashing collages of whatever the new mind-blowing iProduct of the quarter is. The same goes for personal brands; we hear someone's name and a single idea, image or feeling comes to mind.

Michael Jordan
   The Greatest Basketball Player of All Time
Oprah Winfrey
   The Most Powerful Woman in the World
Madonna
   The Genius in Self-Reinvention
Donald Trump
   The Master Businessman
Cornell West
   The Academic
Jay Z
   Music Mogul
Justin Bieber
   Music Prodigy and Teen Heartthrob

15

What You See Is What You Believe

Because a brand is an idea that lives in the mind of the audience, branding aims at creating a better perception, not necessarily a better product.

What does this mean in regard to your personal brand?
It means that your job is to tweak the presentation of your attributes and abilities in a way that creates the best perception in the minds of your audience.

Think About IT: **You get to a basketball game, locate your section, and see that your seats are in the middle of the row. You overhear a rude remark by a man, seated in the row, that he is tired of having to get up and down for the people in the middle.**

Automatically, your perception of this man, a man you have never met before, nor know anything about, is negative. Maybe he just had a bad day? Maybe he recently had knee surgery and is in pain with the frequent sitting and standing. The reality? The truth? It is irrelevant. Your first impression tells you that he is grumpy and inconsiderate.

What You See Is What You Believe

Think About IT: The teacher of your college English class repeatedly arrives late, and never apologizes for keeping you waiting or gives you a reason for her tardiness. She rarely has an attendance sheet, and often has to borrow a student's textbook in order to teach the lesson. The following semester, you make sure to avoid taking classes she teaches, and give your friends a heads-up to not take her classes either.

Regardless of the reason for her lateness; perhaps she teaches a class at another campus which overlaps with your class schedule, or she has to pick her daughter up from school on certain days, your perception of your teacher is that of laziness and irresponsibility. Because of this, you take your "business" elsewhere in the future, and tell others to do the same.

Through the branding process, it is essential to keep in mind how you are perceived and how your brand is perceived. While what is believed about someone or something may not actually be true, this belief- or perception- becomes reality. Perception, whether it is positive or negative, is usually the driving force behind people's thoughts and actions. **Perception ignores reality.** Essentially, perception is more real than reality.

These simple scenarios highlight the power of perception. What makes a personal brand so special is that it allows you to control how the world perceives your brand. It molds others thoughts of you, influences people's actions when interacting with you and, as a result, opens or closes doors of opportunity for you. It is important to establish the characteristics, values and experiences that are special to you and alter your personal image so it coincides. The trick is to project your brand as being so unique and original, that others change their perception of you without even realizing it. According to Paul Kedrosky of CNBC TV, "Brand[ing] is everything, and **perception is 90% of a brand.**" Remember, what we see is what we believe.

Gotta Do You!

As mentioned before, branding is about creating a better perception, not creating a better product. There is this notion that branding is all about changing who you are in order to fit others' expectations. It is not that at all. You have to be YOU. Personal branding is about sincerity. After all, what will be so special about your brand is that it is yours. It is real. It is authentic. People will appreciate, respond more positively and easily relate to the quirks, valuable experiences and strengths that are unique to you if you do not try to hide them and be something that you are not. These idiosyncrasies will more than likely be the most valuable parts of your brand, and can create opportunities and relationships.

"Brand[ing] is everything, and perception is 90% of a brand."
-Paul Kedrosky, CNBC TV

TIMEOUT!

So, you're saying that I can't ever swear, or play pranks on my friends, or have my own opinions anymore?

Absolutely NOT! We are not telling you to change anything about yourself. You can still do all those things. We are just saying that there is a time and a place for everything. When you are in a position that has potential to advance your career, whether it be in your job or school, you should flaunt the professional components of your brand that cater to the people you are around, saving those "off the clock" components for your friends.

You Deserve An Audience!

Without an audience to perform for, what's the use? A key factor in having your brand perceived positively is understanding your intended audience. Regardless of how amazing your brand is, if you don't understand what appeals to your target audience, your brand will fall flat. Remember: the goal of branding is to create positive perceptions, and the target of those positive perceptions is an audience with similar interests and goals as yours. This also includes the ones that you are trying to become a part of. You want to give the people in this audience a reason to want to work with you, interview you, hang out with you, or help you.

19

Why is Personal Branding Important?

Two words: Fat Wallet. Do you like money? Exactly. A personal brand will open doors to new opportunities and help you build relationships with people that are able to help you capitalize on those opportunities.

Branding = Opportunities = Money.

Ever heard of the phrase time equals money? Literally, yes it does. Everything you do requires time of some sorts. As you get a clearer picture in your mind of what your brand is you will begin to be able to identify where your time should be best spent. In running a business for example, rarely do you ever see the CEO answer general phone calls or dealing with the smaller tasks. There is a receptionist or assistant that handles that. The CEO attends the big ticket meetings and handles the larger issues. Guess who gets paid more- a lot more? Yes, the CEO! His time in regards to money is valued more than that of the assistant. Think about that and relate it to your brand.

Recall that we said everyone has a brand but not all brands are created equal. If you treat your personal brand as a multi-million dollar empire compared to a local store, your time should be spent differently.

When you **start thinking of your personal brand as a business** everything is equated to a per hour bases. You can track the time loss or profited by sitting around for an hour watching TV compared to meeting with someone to be apprenticed in a hobby you enjoy. It is possible to track to the second how much time you spend and your overall personal branding bank. Sit and think about that for minute.

In your 24 hours today, **is your personal branding bank in the red?**

The more money you are striving to achieve in life is directly related to the way you treat your brand. Start thinking of yourself as a business and your financial portion of your personal brand building will have the foundation to reap long term rewards.

Wrap Up:

- You ARE a brand! Define your brand on your terms. Not someone else's.
- Your personal branding relies on perception versus reality.
- Personal Branding = Opportunities = Money
- Branding is form of marketing and sales. Learn how to sell your personal attributes as a skill.
- As you create your brand, always keep in mind to remain authentic.

Exercises:

- Make a list of brands that you can relate to. What do you like and dislike about these brands? Relate them to your own definition of your personal branding.

_____
_____
_____
_____

- List your personal goals. How can identifying your brand now help you achieve those goals?

_____
_____
_____
_____

- If you were a personal branding giant what would your title tag be?

_____
_____
_____
_____

- What are some things about the current state of your brand that you would like to improve?

_____
_____
_____
_____

21

Unscramble some key words from this section of the book. As you secure the correct answers, think about what this means in terms of branding yourself.

rngdnabi	_____
odgo	_____
dba	_____
estioivp	_____
aeevigtn	_____
rnaoutipte	_____
aieccicrsahsttr	_____
anemtl maieg	_____
zeaeogbnlcir	_____
leetablra	_____
sisllk	_____
deai	_____
cmlaeih dnjroa	_____
rhopa	_____
yjaz	_____
andnmao	_____
noaldd umtrp	_____
veelieb	_____
ieertcnopp	_____
ratyeil	_____
fesinlecnu	_____
eelards	_____
flowreslo	_____
tseniicry	_____
ihittycatnue	_____
tinpertusopio	_____
rreeca	_____

Chapter 2

Your Personal Branding Arsenal

"It isn't until you come to a spiritual understanding of who you are- not necessarily a religious feeling, but deep down, the spirit within- that you can begin to take control."
-Oprah Winfrey

What you'll learn in this chapter:

- The four categories of personal branding components
- The importance of differentiation
- How to build your personal branding platform

IMAGINE PUTTING A PUZZLE TOGETHER ...

You open the box, dump the contents onto the table and set the box in front of you. Looking back and forth between the pile of tiny pieces and the picture on the front of the box, it is hard to imagine how one will become the other. However, you separate the pile into two categories: edge pieces and middle pieces, systematically connect one piece to the next, and before you know it, you have built a successful, complete puzzle. **Building your brand is very similar.** Just as a whole puzzle is constructed from many pieces, a whole brand is constructed from many personal parts too. As you explore all the possible personal pieces that can be worked into your brand, you will see that they can be broken into four main categories:

Personality: Your unique traits, sense of humor, your attitude towards life, your behavior, the way you communicate

Background: Where you are from, grew up, went to school, what your family is like, stories from your life.

Interests: Hobbies, passions, favorites (books, music, artists, movies, etc.), pastimes, activities.

Lifestyle: Where you live, what you drive, what you eat, what you wear, what you do.

The contents of each of these branding categories will be different for everyone, therefore making them personal. After all, that is your goal: to build your **Personal Brand**. After you separate these four categories, you will be able to begin putting together the personal pieces of your brand puzzle.

Your personality is one of the key weapons in your personal branding arsenal. Regardless of how cliché it may sound, you can tell a lot about a person through their personality. Your personality reflects the type of person you are.

Think about it: You like your friends because of their personality. The traits you appreciate about them either reflect parts of your own personality, or are traits that you simply find attractive and enjoyable to be around. Similarly, upon meeting someone new, you are able to tell whether you will like them based on how they display their personality the first time you meet.

Personality can encompass many things: your sense of humor, your catch phrases, your habits, whether you are shy or outgoing, your views towards religion, whether you take charge or follow in line, how you react under pressure, and so on. Almost any aspect of your behavior can be classified as personality, and worked into your brand.

Your personality acts as a magnet, attracting others to your brand- or repelling them. It helps others decide whether they would want to spend time with you, work with you, support you, have to rely upon you, or offer an opportunity to you.

HOW CAN YOUR BRAND BE
PERSONAL
WITHOUT
PERSONALITY?

Do not forget that you have an audience! It is imperative to be sure that the aspects of your personality that you are incorporating into your personal brand are appropriate for your target audience. Losing opportunities because of inappropriate behavior is something that could be easily avoided by simply taking the time to make sure that the parts of your personality in your brand suit the situations in which you envision yourself.

Understand your target audience and their expectations. You will understand how much and the intensity of your personality to add to your brand. For example, if your goal is to become a rock musician, you need a charismatic, adventurous personality. However, if you aim towards being a lawyer, a wild, rambunctious personality would be completely inappropriate in most cases.

Consider These Personality Tips:

1 Be conservative with your personality when entering a new situation, and as you get a feel for the enviroment and the people in it, adjust the "volume" accordingly.

2 Once you have an established brand, don't be shy. People will recognize, appreciate and expect that bold personality to shine!

Be Forward About Your Background

Another powerful weapon in the building- and continued execution- of your personal brand is your background. Where you are from, where you went to school, your ethnicity, ancestry, personal experiences and stories from your life are key parts of making your brand relatable and interesting to others. People look to these things to gain an understanding of who you are, and why you might do some of the things you do.

Using an aspect of your background as a conversation starter is a useful technique to open yourself to potential opportunities. For example, let us say you are interviewing for a summer internship. On your interviewer's desk, you notice a frame containing a picture of her on a safari in Africa, reminding you of your own safari trip a few years prior. Offering your interviewer the story of your visit to Africa gives them the chance to develop a connection with you, probably heightening the chances that they will offer you the internship opportunity.

Consider These Background Tips:

1 Do your homework. Try to find out about the person you are interviewing with or the company. See if you share any commonalities with them. Learning about their background will help you decide which parts of yours to share.

2 Unless it directly relates to the conversation or situation, stay away from sad stories. You want people to be excited with you, not feel obligated to join your pity party.

3 Be detailed and enthusiastic! People love a good story.

27

They're Interested In Your Interests

Weapon number three is interests. Interests can include hobbies, sports you play or just like to watch, music you listen to, the affinity for cooking or theatre, your passion for animals, movies or TV shows. Interests are a good way to differentiate yourself just enough to be unique, but not so much as to alienate your audience. Although everyone has a different set of interests, sharing a common interest with possible bosses, coaches, teammates, interviewers, or fans is a powerful bonding opportunity and a quick way to get your foot in the door.

Bottom Line:

If you are an artist, build a personal brand that has paintings and drawings as an integral component.
If you play basketball, you would be cutting yourself short by failing to include that as part of your brand.

1 As true with everything else, be very aware of your target audience when sharing your personal Interests. Not all people or organizations are receptive to information about all of your hobbies. Sharing stories about your crazy paint ball trips will likely come as a turn off to the elementary school teacher you are trying to work with.

2 If you do not share the same interest as your target, try to find one that compliments one of theirs. For example, if your target annually vacations in Florida, you might offer a story about your affinity of warm weather.

3 Stay focused. While interests are a good way to create an initial bond, and maintain that bond throughout your relationship, you do not want your extracurricular activities to appear to be more a priority than your work.

4 Be real! If you do not have any interest in something, do not pretend you do. If it is not obvious now, it will be later. And it does not have to be a bad thing; Introducing someone to something new can be a bonding mechanism in itself.

29

Finally, lifestyle is a way to forge a connection with people who do not live like you, but may want to- or conversely, that you do not live like, but you would want to. This is the most important branding component when it comes to personal brands that are in the public eye. By working with you, hanging out with you, being a fan of yours or following you in the media, they are able to get a secondhand feeling of what your life might be like. For example, if you envy the charity work that Angelina Jolie does, you might be inspired to volunteer at an orphanage or animal shelter. While you still do not know Angelina personally, you now share a common bond with her through your charity work.

If you have ever heard the saying "actions speak louder than words" but never had a chance to use it, here is your opportunity. Your lifestyle includes where you live, what you eat, what type of car you drive, your sexual orientation, what clothes you wear and the places you

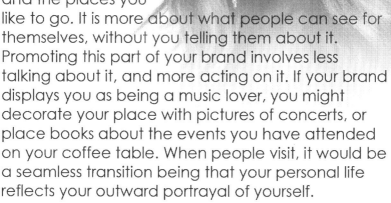

like to go. It is more about what people can see for themselves, without you telling them about it. Promoting this part of your brand involves less talking about it, and more acting on it. If your brand displays you as being a music lover, you might decorate your place with pictures of concerts, or place books about the events you have attended on your coffee table. When people visit, it would be a seamless transition being that your personal life reflects your outward portrayal of yourself.

Consider These Lifestyle Tips:

1 Some people may refuse to work or be associated with you because of where you live or what you look like. Beware of what is expected in your target audience and brand accordingly.

2 Living certain lifestyles to the extreme can appear as showing off. Be careful not to leave a sour taste in your audience's mouth by flaunting your assets.

3 Don't be something you're not. Don't present yourself to be an aspiring professional athlete and always be lazy and overweight.

Truth or DARE?

Ok, I dare you to be different. People do not dare you to do things that are easy; it is hard to stick your neck out and be different from everyone else. Embracing our differences and standing out in the crowd goes against our natural tendencies to want to blend in with our surroundings. **It is time to step out of your comfort zone**, because the truth is that your personal brand will be completely worthless if you do not differentiate yourself from your competitors. There are other people just like you, doing exactly what you are doing, trying to get to the exact same place as you. What do you think differentiates the ones that get there and those who do not?

TIMEOUT! **Many times in your life, you are in a direct line of competition with comparable personal brands. Take a moment and consider this when those points occur. At the very same intersection where you meet your competitors, will you be turning right with the masses, or diverting on the left for a path of your own?**

Consider this scenario. You made the first cut for an open internship in a field you are interested in working. All the candidates have comparable lifestyles and level of education. Before the interview, you take the chance and garner the nerve to drop off samples of your work or you mail in a video that showcase your skill. Simply by making an extra effort, you have already put a positive and impressive message about yourself with the prospective employer. The others did the norm of waiting to bring in samples. You went the extra mile. Who do you think has a better chance of nailing the position?

Wrap Up:

- The four major parts of a brand are: personality, background, interests and lifestyle.
- There is a time and place for everything. Keep in mind your actions and base them on the situation you are in.
- Research is key. The more you are aware of a situation, the better equipped you are with handling it.
- Your current circumstances do not define you.
- Embrace what makes you different.

Exercises:

- List 6-8 points of the portions of your brand: personality, background, interests and lifestyle. These are the basis of your personal brand building puzzle. Does anything stand out?

_____

_____

_____

_____

- Are there personal stories or events that have happened to you that gives you an edge? List them. Remember them for later on.

_____

_____

_____

_____

- Define your target audience. Who are the people that currently relate to your brand? What type of people would you like to include in your audience in the future?

_____

_____

_____

_____

Take a break and view this word search as a rest stop to focus on important key words in Chapter 2. As you circle the words, ask yourself how do these words compliment you.

B. ME Chapter 2:
Your Personal Branding Arsenal

BRANDING   LIFESTYLE
CONTROL   BEHAVIOR
DIFFERENTIATION   TARGET AUDIENCE
COMMUNITY   BOLD
CHARITY   CONVERSATION
UNIQUE   HOMEWORK
TRAITS   ENTHUSIASTIC
COMMUNICATION   BOND
PERSONALITY   REAL
INTERESTS   CONNECTION
BACKGROUND   COMFORT ZONE

S	E	I	A	C	L	O	N	E	S	I	A	T	O	C	N	T
H	L	H	D	S	T	B	A	C	K	G	R	O	U	N	D	T
T	S	O	G	I	T	H	I	N	E	T	A	R	O	S	O	N
T	R	M	R	P	E	R	S	O	N	A	L	I	T	Y	E	E
E	C	E	N	T	H	U	S	I	A	S	T	I	C	W	T	O
C	N	W	E	I	N	Y	Y	T	S	A	A	O	T	N	D	T
B	Y	O	I	L	C	O	U	A	C	R	M	I	C	L	T	N
O	F	R	I	N	Y	O	C	I	T	M	S	M	O	D	T	A
C	B	K	E	T	L	T	N	T	U	T	L	B	M	E	E	R
R	H	Q	I	E	A	U	S	N	S	A	O	E	F	B	N	T
R	D	A	Y	A	M	S	I	E	E	O	C	H	O	R	D	C
R	S	N	R	M	O	T	R	R	F	C	B	A	R	A	C	I
M	N	D	O	I	Y	E	I	E	O	I	T	V	T	N	D	E
Y	D	C	N	B	T	T	I	F	V	O	L	I	Z	D	E	O
E	U	Q	I	N	U	Y	R	F	M	N	G	O	O	I	E	F
A	O	N	I	T	R	I	D	I	E	L	O	R	N	N	T	K
T	A	R	G	E	T	A	U	D	I	E	N	C	E	G	T	I

Chapter 3

Developing Your Brand

"A brand that captures your mind gains behavior. A brand that captures your heart gains commitment."

-Scott Talgo,
Brand Strategist

What you will do in this chapter:

- Complete the self-discovery questionnaire to determine what's important to you
- Answer the brand-discovery questionnaire to begin building your brand
- Determine what you feel your brand is
- Establish your brand characteristics
- Reflect on comparable personal brands to your own

Now is the time to put what you have learned into motion and find out exactly who you are, where you are right now, and what your goals are for the future. It seems like the answer to "Who are you?" would come easily, almost as if we were born knowing exactly who we are. After all, should we not know ourselves better than anyone knows us? The truth is, most people do not truly know who they are or what they really want until they sit down and take the time to discover themselves. This self-discovery process is important because the aspects you determine to be valuable parts of your life, goals, and personality will help you figure out how to construct your personal brand.

I am...Me

Lucky for you, we've collected a list of questions that will help you determine who you are as a person:

PERSONALITY TRAITS

SKILLS

PASSIONS

GOALS

Discover

Ask Yourself: Who am I as a Person?

(1) What are the top 5 personality traits that I'd use to describe myself?

_____
_____
_____
_____

(2) What are the top 5 personality traits that others would use to describe me?

_____
_____
_____
_____

(3) I feel that my most unique or interesting attribute is:

_____
_____
_____
_____

(4) What am I most passionate about in life?

_____
_____
_____
_____

(5) What are my strongest skills? My weakest?

_____
_____
_____
_____
_____

(6) If I could improve 3 things about myself, they would be:

_____
_____
_____
_____
_____

(7) What are my goals for myself in a year? Five years? Ten years?

_____
_____
_____
_____
_____

(8) What is my idea of success? Why?

_____
_____
_____
_____
_____

GET ON THE BRAND-WAGON

After you have figured out what is truly important to you and a little more about who you are as a person, you need to figure out what you want your brand to tell the world. Think of other brands that you have come across and admire. Or do not admire, for that matter. Keeping in mind aspects of other people's brands that you like or dislike will help steer you in the right direction towards developing an effective personal brand that you are proud of. Keep this in mind when answering the following about your brand.

ASK YOURSELF: WHO AM I AS A BRAND?

(1) What are my goals for my brand?

_____

_____

_____

(2) Who is my target audience? Why?

_____

_____

_____

(3) What brand elements do I think my target audience would respond positively to?

_____

_____

_____

(4) What brand elements do I think my target audience would respond negatively to?

_____

_____

_____

(5) What brand elements would best showcase my personality, skills and goals? Why?

_____

_____

_____

_____

(6) Which personal brands do I think are successful? Why?

_____

_____

_____

_____

NOW is the time to announce BRAND YOU!

My Personal Brand is:

_____
_____
_____

3 Supporting Characteristics:

1. _____
_____

2. _____
_____

3. _____
_____

Similar Personal Brands are:

_____
_____
_____

3 Supporting Characteristics:

1. _____
_____

2. _____
_____

3. _____
_____

Wrap Up:

- Understanding who you are in descriptive words helps you to better communicate your brand.
- Take the time to discover and be in tune with yourself, your goals and your brand.
- Creating a brand takes time. It doesn't happen overnight. The more time and effort you put in to it, the further along your brand will be.

Exercises:

- After reviewing your Who am I Questionnaire, define yourself in one sentence.

_____

_____

_____

_____

- Does your *Who Am I* **as a brand** and *Who am I* **as a Person** Questionnaire match up? Are there inconsistencies? Make note of them for future reference as you continue.

_____

_____

_____

_____

- After collecting your raw data, name a personal and product brand that relates well to you. Do the successes and failures of these brands match what you would like to have for your own?

_____

_____

_____

_____

Across:

1. A part of your personality: funny, ambitious, outgoing, energetic, shy, etc.
5. "What we see is what we _____."
7. It is important to use the categories in your personal branding arsenal to create this with your audience.
9. The most important branding component when it comes to personal brands that are in the spotlight.
10. Having this type of personal brand will help to open doors of opportunity.
12. A _____ brand creates an immediate idea in your mind.
13. "_____ your brand, or it will _____ you."
14. Plans that you set for yourself towards.
18. Where you are from, where you went to school, what your family is like, past experiences, etc., all fall into this branding category.
20. Share this about yourself in order to make a connection with others during an interview or for networking purposes.
21. Being this goes against our natural tendencies to want to blend into the crowd, but it is an essential part of your brand.
22. What is immediately formed when you think of a brand.
23. Something that is special about you, making you different from everyone else.

Down:

2. Every component of your personal brand needs to have a clear, specific target in order to make it as successful as possible.
3. "The powerful, clear, positive idea that comes to mind when people think of you."
4. The hobbies or activities that you enjoy doing.
6. A strong brand makes you more _____ to potential employers, coaches, teachers, etc.
8. Achieving this is one of the main reasons to have a strong personal brand.
11. Things that you do well and that should be accented in your brand.
15. True or not, it is a person's outlook on reality.
16. A brand that is real and unique to you is _____.
17. A collection of skills, characteristics, slogans and logos used to entice an audience to a brand.
19. Always have this in mind when building and executing your brand.

Building your brand should Be FUN! Let's see how good you've gotten with learning the concepts.

Branding Crossword Puzzle

Part 2:

Executing Your Personal Brand

"**A brand is a living entity** - and it is enriched or undermined cumulatively over time, the product of a thousand small gestures."

-**Michael Eisner**
former CEO of Disney

Chapter 4

Communicating Your Brand

What you'll learn in this chapter:

- The importance of effectively communicating your brand
- Tips for enhancing your speech communication
- Types of interviews
- Tips for promoting your brand through your interview answers
- How to network efficiently

Bottom Line:

EFFECTIVE COMMUNICATION IS AN ESSENTIAL PART OF BUILDING AND MAINTAINING YOUR PERSONAL BRAND.

Whether you are hanging out with friends at a bowling alley, participating in class discussions, going on a college tour, speaking on the phone, or doing an interview for a job, school or sports, you must always be mindful of the way you communicate. What do I mean by "the way you communicate," you ask? The way you speak and write, your body language, how you dress, and your attitude all fall into this category. The things listed help people form their opinion of you. As we mentioned before, perception is everything. Do not ever lose sight of that. It takes someone just three to five seconds to form a perception, or first impression, of you.

"Through effective communication, you can build credibility, network effectively, and earn the trust and respect of those whose opinions really matter."
-Dan Schawbel, personal branding guru

One of the most important methods of communication is speaking. Having a strong interpersonal skill set is not only one of the first steps in getting people to have confidence in your brand, but it is also among the most desired skill set in a professional industry. Just as products and companies use ads or commercials to "speak" to us and promote their brands, you must be mindful of the way you speak and do the same for your brand.

Each time you give a speech, a presentation, an interview or have a normal, day-to-day conversation, you need to think of it as your own personal branding commercial. Are you portraying your brand in the way you would like to be perceived? While each and every interaction is a valuable opportunity to showcase your personal brand in a positive light, it is also important to remember that your credibility is at risk during each of these interactions.

For example, using profanity, speaking in a monotone and uninterested voice, or not fully answering questions are easy ways to kill your credibility in the eyes of your audience. If you have a conversation with a professor who is talking in a monotone voice, yawning, and saying "uhh..." every 30 seconds, you probably will lose interest in what is being said and think that he is not knowledgeable of what he is talking about. The same goes for you too. Simply put, if you do not sound like you know what you are talking about, your audience is going to assume you are clueless. If you do not seem like you care what you are talking about, your audience is going to think you could care less.
Perception IS reality.

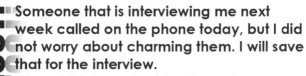

Someone that is interviewing me next week called on the phone today, but I did not worry about charming them. I will save that for the interview.

Wrong! It is important to always be prepared, professional, and well spoken, whether it be in person, on the phone, through video chat, or another method of communication. Just because you may not be face to face with the person you are communicating with does not mean that you are off the hook. **Remember**: View every interaction with other people as an opportunity to reach your goals. Because of this, you must always be sure that your personal brand shines so others are attracted to YOU- the life line of your brand!

Do Your Audience Homework

Remember how we talked about finding your target audience in chapter one? Let us see how well you grasped that concept. Because different forms of communication apply to different audiences, it is important to be able to determine what type of category that person falls into. Be aware of the type of communication mediums that are appropriate.

Do your homework before approaching them. You might contact someone in a less formal way. For example, a club president. It would be okay to contact them using instant messaging or a social media network. In the case of people such as interviewers, professors, and coaches, always make sure to be more professional and contact by phone or email. By doing this research, you will be sure that you are communicating in a way that is most   convenient for them. People love when they do not have to do the "leg work". Try to communicate in a way that will work to your best advantage.

CONSIDER THESE TIPS:

1

LISTEN

Oral communication is not only about what you say. Be sure to listen carefully to what people are saying to you in order to gather important information about your audience. Make a note of important verbal signals such as facts, details or directions. By listening effectively, you might find conversation starters for your next encounter and you will be sure to meet all expectations of your counterpart.

2

TAKE YOUR TIME

Allow your audience to effectively listen to you. Pace yourself and speak in a manner that best makes it easiest for them to soak in all the facts, details and directions that you are trying to convey. Make sure they have a thorough understanding of the subject matter, answering questions or promising to get back to them if you need to do follow-up research.

3

ASK QUESTIONS

It is better to ask questions from the get-go and make sure you understand every part of a conversation, or all directions to a task you are supposed to complete than to play a guessing game with yourself later. It is more embarrassing to fail to complete a task later because you misunderstood something than to ask a bunch of questions when it is assigned. Asking questions is also a key technique to show that you are engaged in and care about what the other person in the conversation has to say. A general rule of thumb is to always ask at least one question after all communication. It is often helpful to make a list of possible questions to ask prior to entering an important conversation. This shows preparedness and interest on your part!

Consider These Tips:

USE YOUR BODY

4

When engaging in a conversation with someone, spoken words are not the only way you are communicating. Be sure that your body language mimics what you are saying, by stressing important points with hard gestures, and stimulating your audience with facial expressions. Even further, be sure to pick up on your counterpart's body language as well and adjust accordingly.

BE INTERESTING

5

Increase the interest and engage your audience by enunciating your words and speaking dynamically and professionally. Animated people automatically grab the attention of their audience and allow them to feel a connection and a strong confidence in them. When people are interested in what you have to say and have confidence in the subject on which your are speaking, it means that they have invested their trust in you and your brand. They might be more willing to help you in the future.

Interviews àre one of the most important times to pay attention to your verbal communication, making sure you are clear, professional and engaging. After all, one of the main reasons for building yourself a personal brand is to open the door to opportunities. Interviewing is the first step towards capitalizing on the opportunities that your brand has made available to you. Throughout life, you will have more interviews than you might realize. Whether you recognize them as interviews or not, so-called "casual" conversations with someone you meet at a banquet, or a phone call with a friend of your boss are both examples of conversations that might classify as interviews. An interview is qualified as a conversation during which information is gathered and conclusions are drawn of one or more of the participants. With that definition imagine how many "interviews" you have had in your lifetime.

TIME OUT!

You keep mentioning that we have to be professional and speak professionally all the time. Does this mean we always have to be super-serious?

Absolutely not. By reinforcing that you must pay attention to your professionalism, we do not mean that you have to be straight faced and down to business during every second of an interview or conversation. By "professional," we just mean that you need to keep in mind that your brand is always being evaluated by the people you encounter, so you should present yourself in a way that is pleasing to your audience. You can still be professional while laughing or making appropriate jokes, as long as your behavior is modest and accepted by the type of audience you are surrounded by. Also, laughing with your counterpart and sharing jokes are good ways of keeping the interest level high and creating a comfortable environment for your engagement. The more opportunity you give yourself to smile, it gives the illusion that you are approachable and makes the situation more at ease.

Types of Interviews

Media: Television, Radio, Print (Magazines, Newspapers, Brochures), Online (Blogs, Online Papers, Social Media)

Professional: Jobs, Internships, Volunteer work, Company Promotions

Academic: Four-Year Colleges, Technical Schools, Scholarships, Trade Schools (the Arts, Mechanics, etc.)

Recruiting: Military, Army, Navy, ROTC, Army Reserves

Auditions: Musical, Theatre (Acting), Athletic, Public Speaking

"**Luck** has nothing to do with it, because I have spent many, many hours, countless hours, **working** for my one moment in time, not knowing when it would come."
-Serena Williams

Be Prepared or Be Dismissed

Whether you are engaging in one of these "casual" interviews, or attending a more formal job or college interview, it is imperative that you do your homework and come prepared to the conversation. Being unprepared for an interview can be extremely harmful to your brand and your career. Poor speech, slang language and careless answers to questions can all be detrimental to your brand, helping you to close the door to a potential opportunity rather than open it. How do you avoid these kinds of speech mishaps? Well, remember when you were little and your mom told you that practice makes perfect? You got it... She was right! Practice and preparation are your key to making sure you have got all your communication corners covered.

Not only is it important to be prepared by practicing your speech, but it is just as important to prepare yourself with information on the organization, and people, with whom you are interviewing. Entering a job interview with little to no knowledge of the company will almost automatically cross you off your potential employer's list of candidates for the position. Know what you are talking about, be excited about your words and ask questions to enhance your knowledge. Consider the following chart for tips on how to answer some typical interview questions in a way that will best benefit your personal brand.

Standard Interview Questions

Question:	What to keep in mind when responding:
How would you describe yourself?	List the top characteristics of your personal brand. Note: Make sure these characteristics are ones that the organization you are interviewing with will find useful.
How would others describe you?	Similar answer to above, but list different top characteristics of your brand, only repeating one or two.
What are your strengths and weaknesses?	Rather than listing personality traits, list abilities that correspond with your overall brand. For example, you might say you are very organized. For weaknesses, try to look for something that can be spun as a positive. For example, you might say you are a perfectionist, which throws your time management off at times.
What are your goals?	If you are interviewing for a school, your answer should include something about that institution. Same goes for interviewing for a job with a company, team, etc.

Standard Interview Questions

Question:	What to keep in mind when responding:
Describe how you handled a difficult situation.	Describe a scenario that includes how you used one of the strengths you mentioned before.
Do you prefer to work individually or as part of a team?	Any organization, whether it be a school, a job, a sport, etc. that you interview with will demand that you work well both individually and as a team.

You may want to mention that you work specifically well individually, which helps you to become a leader when working with a team. |
What does 'success' mean to you?	Define success to reflect your goals and tie them in to the information you found about the interviewer from your research.
Why do you want to work at this company/go to this school/be a part of this organization?	Be genuine and speak honestly. Try touching on personal reasons versus answers you think the interviewer wants to hear.
What motivates you?	Always use your personal experiences to answer this question and similar ones like it.

Standard Interview Questions

Question:	What to keep in mind when responding:
How do you work under pressure? **10**	No one is perfect. Letting your interviewer know what makes you tick will better help them evaluate you. Be truthful.
Would you rather work for the money or the satisfaction? **11**	Life is about a balance. Practice answers for both.
Are you ready to take on the pressure of playing in this league/ working with this company/ attending this school? **12**	You should not be interviewing if you are not ready for dealing with pressure. Proudly say yes and list reasons why.

SportsCenter, Facebook, Clear Channel, Wallstreet Journal, Sports Illustrated, Twitter, Perez Hilton, TMZ, ESPN Magazine, The Daily News... You will most likely recognize these names as some of your daily go-to sources for information on a variety of topics. Breaking news, scandals, rumors, secrets, tips, emergencies, gossip; the media covers all topics, all people... everything. Once something hits the media- which is updated by the second- it goes viral, allowing people worldwide in on the news.

The term "mass media" refers to any source used to relay information and there are four main mass media outlets: television, radio, print and online. While media is a wonderful thing as far as entertainment and news are concerned, it can be tricky to determine the real truth in a story through any given source.

For example, let us say you and your friend attended a girls soccer game last weekend and witnessed the coach yelling aggressively at the players during the game. After the game, you both inform your parents of the events that transpired. You tell them that the team did a great job and the coach really cares about winning and motivated them to do their best. However, your friend tells his parents that the coach is verbally abusive to the players on his team. The same experience with the same basic facts spawned two completely different stories. Maybe your friend was on a team with an overly aggressive coach before, making him sensitive towards this soccer coach. Maybe his sister was a victim of verbal abuse, therefore making him cautious of the coach's behavior towards the girls soccer team. Regardless of the reasoning, a person's beliefs and values affect the stories they tell, thus molding the listener's perception of what is real.

This holds true for the media as well. The media is able to place their own perceptions and beliefs on the topics they cover; therefore, it carries a lot of weight in molding the publics' idea of reality.

Standard Interview Questions

Duh, we all know this. But why is this important for me to know right now?

Whether you are going to be playing in tournaments, speaking at college events, performing in concerts, volunteering for a charity organization, etc., you may be the subject of the media spotlight at some point, and you want to make sure to present your brand as accurately and positively as possible.

Are you ready 2 interview?

Ask Yourself: Am I ready for an interview?

(1) Which of the interview types might best apply to you at this point in your life?

_____

_____

_____

(2) What kinds of interviews have you been through before?

_____

_____

_____

(3) Do you think these interviews were successful? Why or why not?

_____

_____

_____

(4) Pretend you're in an interview right now. Describe how you have handled a difficult situation in your life.

_____

_____

_____

(5) What aspect of your speech do you think you need to work on the most?

_____

_____

_____

(6) What aspects of your speech do you think you do best? Why?

_____

_____

_____

_____

_____

Do the Neck-Work to Grow Your Network

If you happen to meet someone at an event, it is a good idea to connect with them on Facebook as a follow-up to your in-person meeting. Whether it be a simple "hello" or "it was nice to meet you," following up with people after you meet them in person is an essential part of building relationships. Invite a call to action, enticing new people to do the same with you.Create personal business cards and carry them with you at all times.

Consider the following Do's and Don'ts of networking to make sure you are making the most of your opportunities.

"In-person networking is the ultimate form of brand building if you're networking with the right people."
-David Kirkpatrick
Senior Editor, Fortune

CORRECTLY

how to network

- Make a strong and favorable first impression.
- Try to remember the name of the person you are speaking with and at least 3 facts about them.
- Be conscious of people's feelings and reactions when speaking with them.
- Find creative ways to give value or promote other individuals, as they will reciprocate.

- Be an active listener and take genuine interest in what others have to say.

- Always introduce yourself with your name and a firm handshake when meeting people.

- Maintain strong eye contact.

- Follow up with people you have met and express your interest in keeping in touch and meeting again at a later date.

INCORRECTLY

how to network

- Interrupt a conversation and force your way into it.
- Ask for an internship or job without even introducing yourself.
- Fail to make proper eye contact or give a firm handshake when meeting someone.
- Wear a short skirt, jeans, gym shorts or other inappropriate clothing to a formal meeting, event or interview.
- Treat a new contact like a stranger instead of forming a relationship.
- Forget your resume or other important materials at home, thinking the other person will remember your name and contact information.
- Say you are to busy to help someone else, yet ask that person to support you.
- Position yourself as a superior to your manager or coworkers.
- Have poor posture and no confidence.

Wrap Up:

- Always remember the phrase: "Perception is everything."
- Communication is the key to ensure that you have a strong personal brand.
- The way you speak and interact with people reflects in a positive or negative way about your brand.
- Know what type of audience you are speaking to and communicate accordingly.
- Research the organization (or people) you are interviewing with beforehand to ensure you have information to communicate effectly.
- When communicating:
  1. Listen 2. Take Your Time
  3. Use Your Body 4. Be Interesting

Exercises:

- Answer the standard interview questions. Write them down. Practice your delivery of the answers often until you feel confident. Try it with a friend and have them critique you on delivery and your body language. The more you do it, the better you will become. Critique yourself here:

_____
_____
_____
_____
_____
_____
_____
_____
_____

Test your knowledge of this chapter's content by matching these words with the correct phrases. Draw a line to the correct answer.

Communication is an essential part of ...

networking.

What people may perceive your brand as, is set by ...

are tips for communicating effectively.

Confidence in yourself helps people ...

ensures you will be prepared for the conversation.

Listening, taking your time, asking questions, using your body language and always being interested ...

first impressions.

your Personal Brand.

A conversation during where information is gathered and conclusions are drawn amongst the participants ...

believe in your brand.

qualifies as an interview.

Researching and being informed prior to a meeting or inter-view ...

To increase your net worth for your branding communicating your brand is essential for ...

Chapter 5

Appearance

"You now have to decide what 'image' you want for your brand. Image means personality. Products, like people, have personalities, and they can make or break them in the market place."

-David Ogilvy

What you'll learn in this chapter:

- How to dress to support your brand

- How body language affects your brand

- How to have a positive image individually and as a team

So, you have learned what exactly personal branding is and why it is important. We hope the creation process has been a fun one for you so far. As you continue on your path towards developing the strongest, most successful personal brand, there is something new to add to the list: Appearance.

Appearance is comprised of the way you dress, and your body language.

I know, I know...so many things to keep track of, but you never know who you might run into!

As we mentioned before in chapter one, **first impressions** take a second to make, and a lifetime to break. The first impression formed about you will be largely based on your appearance. Therefore, your appearance is a crucial part of the short and long term success, acceptance, and credibility of your brand.

Eye Candy

At first, it might seem shallow to think that what you wear could affect the way you are perceived, but it is true. It is not about what designer names you are wearing or who has on the newest pair of jeans. The focus is more so about dressing in a manner that is appropriate for the situation in which you find yourself.

Specific styles of dress are required for certain situations or events. People moderate their appearance to fit the circumstance. For example, if you show up to a job interview wearing your practice sweats and hunching over in your chair, you will probably be perceived as lazy or careless. Having said that, if you show up to practice wearing a tuxedo and top hat, you still would not make the right impression. You will probably still be perceived as careless, and maybe even rude for not taking the time to properly prepare for the activity in which you will be participating.

You will know what type of dress is appropriate for a given situation by....wait for it.... **understanding your target audience**! If you are not conscious of what type of clothing will most please the audience, your perception is going to plummet. Doing your research, and taking the time to make sure you are appropriately dressed for an event or for a meeting with someone is a key step in assuring your brand will garner positive perception. Take a look at the chart below to see some ways in which people change their attire to fit certain situations.

APPROPRIATE DRESS

SITUATION	
School or Job Interview	**Suit, dress shirt and slacks or blouse and skirt**
Class	Jeans and relaxed shirt
Sporting Event	**Jeans, t-shirt**
Post-Game Interview	Business casual shirt and relaxed pants
Presentation	**Dress pants, button-down shirt or nice blouse and skirt**

Refer back to Chapter 1 where we talked about product branding. We learned how companies use strategies such as clever slogans, and attractive logos, or packaging to grab attention and entice customers into buying their product.

WELL and Think of yourself as the product your appearance as the packaging.

Your packaging should be fresh and calculated, giving off the best reflection of your talents, character and abilities as possible. You want it to grab your audience's attention and make them believe and invest in you as a product.

Non-Verbal Interaction

Regardless of your surroundings, whether you are in a work meeting, giving a class presentation or having lunch with your friends, body language is an essential part of communicating and supporting your brand.

Various research studies show that 45-60 percent of communication consists of body language, or nonverbal communication. Can you believe that? Almost, if not more than, half of the messages we send and receive are interpreted from body posture, gestures, facial expressions, hand movements, arm placement and eye contact. Do you know what this means? Let us keep it simple. It means that no matter how thoughtful you are when choosing your words, if your body language is contradictory to what you are saying, you lose all credibility, and your message is meaningless.

Think back on a few different situations or conversations and envision your body language. Did you come off as defensive because your arms were folded across your chest during a conference with a teacher? Did the college admissions counselor think you were nervous because you lacked steady eye contact when she was talking to you? Maybe the new rookie on your team thought you were being disrespectful when you gave him a careless, weak handshake. Your body language is capable of sending some pretty powerful messages, before you have even opened your mouth to speak.

Check out the following examples of how certain body language can affect the message being sent.

Posture

Body Stance

Message Conveyed

Sitting upright, but not stiff

Comfortable, Confident

Hunched down in chair

Nervousness, lacking confidence, uninterested, careless

Interest, involvement

Leaning angled towards speaker

Standing or sitting too close to counterpart

Pushy, arrogance, overbearing

Stand-offish, timidness, inferiority

Standing or sitting too far away from counterpart

Hand and Arm Gestures

Gesture	Message Conveyed

Hands above the neck, fiddling with face, hair

Nervousness, anxiety, lying

Annoyed, uncertain

Arms up, hands behind head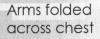

Arms folded across chest

Closed, defensive

Dominance, emphasizing a point, aggressiveness

Hands palms-down on table

Arms down at sides or behind back

Openness, willingness to take on new things, bravery

Eye Contact and Head Positioning

Gesture	Message Conveyed

Gesture

Head slightly
tilted to side

Message Conveyed

Friendly, open

Head looking
straight forward

Self-assured,
authoritative

Interest, engaged in
conversation,
respect

Direct eye contact

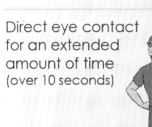

Direct eye contact
for an extended
amount of time
(over 10 seconds)

Challenging, daring,
taunting

Submissiveness,
insincerity,
disengaged in
conversation

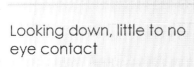

Looking down, little to no
eye contact

Wrap Up:
- Your image is made up of both appearance and body language. They are complimentary and should be reflective of each other, saying the same emotion.
- You only have one time to make a great first impression.
- Dress for the occasion. Ask ahead of time if there is a dress code or requirement.
- Be aware of your body language and what it is conveying to the other person or people you are communicating with.

Exercises:
- Review the clothing that you already own with the idea of what will be appropriate for different situations outlined in the chapter. If you are missing a clothing element, purchase or borrow one so that you are always ready to be dressed appropriately for any occasion.

_____
_____
_____
_____

- Now that you are aware of body language signs and how your appearance can be interpreted, take it out for a test drive. For one week commit to applying some of the rules you have learned. See if you notice any differences with how people treat you.

_____
_____
_____
_____

Let us test your skills in appearance and body language. Based on the situations below, rate the characters from 1-3 (1 being the best, 3 the worst) on which is best prepared for the scenario.

1. You are on your way to a social networking function. It starts at 6:00pm. Most of your close friends will be attending as well.

Character 1   **Character 2**   **Character 3**

2. Good news! You have received a call that your resume has caught the eye of a manager you have been waiting weeks on. With a busy schedule, he invites you to attend an open house for a client to casually interview.

Character 1   **Character 2**

1._____
_____
_____

2._____
_____

Character 3

Chapter 6

Social Media

"Don't say anything online that you wouldn't want plastered on a billboard with your face on it."
— Erin Bury

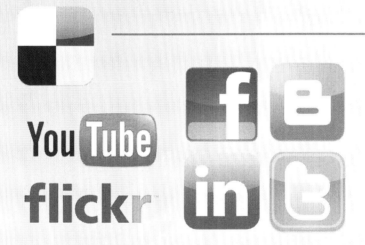

What you'll learn in this chapter:

- How to use social media to endorse and enhance your brand

- Descriptions and tips on using different social media sites

- Positives and Negatives of social media

Frankly, social media has taken over the world. Over the past ten years, social media has infiltrated all facets of society and has revolutionized the way we communicate on all levels. The dramatic decline of mass media, specifically print, such as newspapers and magazines are a direct result of the rapid escalation of social media. Think about it: People used to read their local paper for the latest news headlines; now they find out about current events from reporters' twitter feeds. You used to practically travel, whether short or long distances, to purchase topical magazines to read about the newest cooking tips or music top-ten lists; now they are posted and endorsed all over the internet. Social media is not only useful for news and leisurely information, it also gives people a way to personally interact with others by sharing personal information such as pictures and stories, reconnecting with lost friends and family, and so much more. It has essentially brought people together and strengthened relationships at the simple click of a mouse.

www.BrandingMyselfEveryday.com

Celebrities and Social Media

"How does this apply to personal branding?" you may ask.

Chad Ochocinco
Charlie Sheen
Kim Kardashian
Anderson Cooper
LeBron James

These are just a few examples of the countless celebrity brands that are up to their necks in social media, tweeting, updating statuses and posting pictures numerous times throughout any given day. While it may seem silly for someone like Aston Kutcher to feel the need to tweet about the fantastic dinner he had last night, it is a way of connecting with his fans and followers, forging a special kind of relationship with the public. By posting random updates about daily activities, mentioning personal opinions on movies or music, uploading pictures of their pet or a friendly outing, or offering their side of the story on an issue that may need some clarification, people in the limelight are given a voice through social media. This allows them to take control of managing their own personal brands rather than relying on the media to do so. Social media is unbiased and has leveled the playing field, giving everybody the same technology and capabilities to communicate.

Social Media and YOU

Social media is an integral part of strengthening, endorsing and spreading the word about your personal brand. The majority of us do not have the guidance of a publicist or manager to mediate our social media activity like some of the celebrity brands that we so love to follow. However, it is important to realize that you are your own PR hype machine, the manager of your own brand, and therefore have a responsibility to act, and react, accordingly when engaging in social media. In this case, you are no different than a celebrity. You should use social media to the advantage of your brand, just as the celebrities do for theirs.

Think of your social media pages as your own personal brand billboards. As people on the Facebook highway "drive by" your billboard, they should get a positive and genuine, brief, glimpse into who you are as a person and who you are as a brand. Social media is an invaluable way to connect with people that may be crucial to opening your door to opportunity. Therefore, your goal in using social media is to connect with people, talk about topics, post pictures, comment on posts, and mention headlines that garner the interest and appeal to the people within your target audience. Your Facebook and MySpace pages, Twitter and LinkedIn accounts should be authentic to who you are as a person, having the perfect mix of playfulness and professionalism to attract people with who you may want to network.

Be Consistent!

As your personal brand continues to evolve, you will find that you have both an online network (an online community of people that share the same interests), as well as an offline network (the people you work with, play sports with, go to school with, meet at events, etc.) that are made up of what we have come to know and love as our target audience. Because you are presented with these two separate ways of presenting your brand, the important thing to be aware of when incorporating social media into your branding is consistency. Consistency can make or break your brand credibility.

CONSIDER THIS SCENARIO:

You are the manager at a company that I am trying to get a job with. We meet at a networking event. Wanting you to think that I am reliable and responsible, I tell you that I am relatively reserved and am not someone who likes to go to parties. The next day, on Facebook, you notice that I have a couple of different photo albums with pictures of myself acting crazy and out of control at different events. Would you this still consider me as a candidate for the job remembering our earlier conversation? Probably not.

The inconsistency between what I said to you in person and what you saw on my Facebook page completely ruins my credibility and makes me seem untrustworthy and unprofessional.

Your goal is to ensure there is no disconnect between your offline network and your online network. Your online presence should be a mirror image of your in-person demeanor, with all information, whether formal or informal, being identical. This issue of consistency applies not only between your on- and offline networks, but between your different online interactions as well. In viewing your various social media pages, there may be different types of material present (due to the site you are using), but the general foundation of the information should obviously come from the same place, the same person, the same brand. **In doing this, the branding is consistent.**

Google Yourself!

Let us be honest. Most of us have gotten bored enough to Google ourselves at one point or another. While it can be fun to dig around and see what you can find by searching your name online, it is not an activity meant only for those times when you have nothing else to do. Searching your name online is a good way to make sure your online presence is positive, productive and consistent with your offline presence. Conducting these types of searches will allow you to see, and monitor, anything that includes your name, whether you are the one that posted it to the internet or not. This is also a good way to double check your social media pages, as they will most likely be one of the first things returned in your search. If you decide that something that comes up in your search is not in sync with your general brand, take the steps towards removing it from the web.

Double checking your online presence is also an integral part of making sure you do not unknowingly squash any opportunities that may come your way. The vast majority of employers, teachers, scouts and recruiters conduct online searches prior to extending an opportunity. Why? Because they can. It is easy and effective.

By simply entering your name into the search bar, they are essentially running a preliminary background check on you. If a potential coach were to search your name online before meeting with you and found inappropriate pictures of you, or saw that you posted a variety of profanity-filled status updates to your Facebook page, do you think that would make him more inclined to want you on his team?

Every negative comment, status, and picture has the potential to destroy an opportunity before it is even presented to you. How unfair would it be that you lost an opportunity because you did not follow up and make sure your online brand was not in sync with your offline brand?

Because the internet is such a bottomless, and often permanent, pit of information, it is imperative that you monitor what you post and what is posted about you on all sites, especially your social media pages. View social media as a community, an open network, where you can meet and mingle with people before you even meet them face to face. And vice versa. In person, you would surely think twice about acting inappropriate or saying something negative to someone's face; follow in line with this on your social media pages as well. Your network is no longer just your neighborhood or your school. Social media connects you to the global world, allowing you to think and act in a much larger platform. Consequently, it is imperative that your social media pages responsibly reflect your brand.

Social Media and Networking

Social media is a great way to continue, or begin, your networking efforts, both personally and professionally. It levels the social playing field and knocks down the boundaries between statuses, company, school, or occupational hierarchies, and geographical locations. It gives everyone an equal opportunity to get in touch with each other at the mere click of a mouse. There is no excuse to not take full advantage of using social media to expand your network of contacts.

Another reason social media sites are such helpful networking tools is because they contain simple, but useful information about the people that you have or will be connecting with. Have you ever met someone for the first time, and felt those long, awkward silences that come up while you wrack your brain for something to talk about? Do not be shy, it has happened to all of us. Social media can, to an extent, be a remedy for awkward conversations. If you know ahead of time that you will be meeting with someone, it is a good idea to browse through their social media pages and collect some general information to refer back to during your conversation. If you are meeting with a basketball coach, you might want to see if he has anything on his page about his favorite or least favorite players and teams, what basketball or sports related organizations he is involved in, or what teams he used to play on when he attended school. When one of those awkward silences start to creep into your conversation later, you can fill it by introducing something you found on his page.
Not only will this make your conversation a lot more comfortable, but the person you are meeting with will be impressed that you took the time to get to know a little more about them prior to meeting.

In the same way that you will be doing a little mild stalking of the people you meet with, they will do the same to you. However in this case, not everything is flowers and rainbows and just finding fun facts to talk to you about. You have to be excruciatingly careful about what you post to your social media pages, as this information can make or break an opportunity for you. Sifting through your pages is a way for potential employers, coaches, interviewers, or professors to run their own brief background check on you, at no cost to them.

Studies show that 45% of employers checked candidates' social media pages prior to interviewing them in 2009-2010, which is a statistic that is certainly not shrinking. While most employers have admitted to not using information on social media pages to make a final decision about a candidate, negative information posted surely stays in their minds when weighing multiple people for a position.

Check out the following examples of social media content that real-life employers say have caused them to turn a candidate down ...

- Provocative or inappropriate photographs or information.

- Photos that show drinking or drug use.

- Negative comments about a previous employer, coworkers, clients, coaches, teachers, etc.

- Poor communication skills.

- Discriminatory comments.

- Lied about qualifications or accomplishments.

- Shared confidential information about previous employer, company, coach, school, etc.

You're Gettin' A Background Check

Accordingly, the same study showed that 18% of that same group of employers said that positive and productive content found on candidates' social media pages actually made the employer more fitting to hire them.

Check out some examples of social media content that have helped job candidates win-over potential employers:

- Page reflected the person's personality in a clean polished manner.

- Page displayed the candidate in a way that showed a possible good fit for the position and the company.

- The content reinforced the candidate's qualifications.

- The page was creative.

- Proper communication skills was used throughout.

- Comments from friends were positive and acted as instant references for the candidate.

While this study focused on social media pages being screened by potential employers on the job scene, do not think for a second that coaches, professors, directors, and people in similar positions, do not take the same actions when considering a person for a spot within their organization and groups.

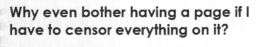

Why even bother having a page if I have to censor everything on it?

Just because there are certain things that you would not want certain people to see, does not in any way, mean that you should throw out the idea of having a social media page altogether. There is this beautiful thing called privacy, and most social media outlets have privacy settings that allow you to block all, none, or some parts of your page to all, none, or some viewers. If you have a few great photo albums of you and your family and you on vacation but have friends that post an inappropriate joke to your page now and then, the privacy settings will allow you to block viewers from seeing what others write to you, while still being able to enjoy your photos. When trying to reach a goal and capitalize on an opportunity, it is essential to make sure the privacy settings on your social media pages are activated. It would be such a shame to lose out on a great opportunity because you did not take those extra two seconds to make your profile private.

Choose Your Privacy Settings

Connecting on Facebook
Control basic information your friends will use to find you on Facebook. View Settings

Sharing on Facebook
These settings control who can see what you share.

		Everyone	Friends of Friends	Friends Only	Other
Everyone					
Friends of Friends	Your status, photos, and posts			*	
Friends Only	Bio and favorite quotations			*	
	Family and relationships		*		
	Photos and videos you're tagged in			*	
Recommended	Religious and political views		*		
Custom ✓	Birthday		*		
	Permission to comment on your posts			*	
	Places you check in to [?]			*	
	Contact information			*	

☑ Let friends of people tagged in my photos and posts see them.

✐ Customize settings   ✅ This is your current setting.

Apps and Websites
Edit your settings for using apps, games and websites.

Block Lists
Edit your lists of blocked people and apps.

Controlling How You Share
Learn more about your privacy on Facebook.

Positives & Negatives, Do's & Don't's, Can's & Can'ts

As with many things, there are appropriate and inappropriate ways to use social media. Your social media pages have the potential to have a huge impact on your personal brand. Because of this, it is important to keep a couple things in mind when using the various social media sites. Check out the following charts to determine whether your social media content is appropriate.

Positives & Negatives of Social Media

Gives you direct contact with fans and followers	Public sites able to be viewed by anyone, anywhere
Allows you to show personality and share personal stories	Negative content stays on sites and may be used to your disadvantage
Allows you to share and/or trade pictures with friends, family and followers	Content can be easily misinterpreted (song lyrics, movie quotes, spelling abbreviations)
Gives you the chance to address rumors	Contact information posted can put you in a vulnerable situation
Promise real-life relationships with those you are connected with on any given social media site	Disconnect with a "real life" connection with people, causing a lack of feeling for the "human touch"

Can Do vs Can't Do

Provide you with a great online networking community	Keep people listening if you have nothing of interest or importance to say
Allow you to stay in contact with friends, family and fans	Force people to take part in your social media activity
Help you connect with people all around the world	Make you an overnight sensation
Give you the authority over your own online brand	Guarantee you will be famous

FACEBOOK

When thinking of social media pages, **Facebook** is probably the first network to come to mind, and probably one in which most, you are already involved. With over **600 million** active users worldwide- of that, an estimated 135.1 million users are from the United States-Facebook is the most widely used social media site.

Upon joining Facebook, users will create a personal profile. In the profile, users may upload information about their job, hometown, education, likes, hobbies, favorite quotes, birthday, contact information, relationship status, and a lot more.

Facebook users connect by "friending" each other, and after friend requests are accepted, all contacts are listed as "friends." Friends are able to communicate with one another through public messaging on the profile wall, private email-like message inboxes, or the live chat feature. Users are able to post comments, pictures, links to websites, or videos to their friends' wall, and every post is able to be commented on. Users are also able to comment on other peoples' comments, or simply "like" someone else's post.

In addition to simply listing likes and dislikes in the personal information section of their page, Facebookers are able to join groups. These groups are similar to clubs, and are focused on almost any subject imaginable. There are groups supporting sports teams, singular athletes, TV shows, events, movies, people. There are activist groups focused on animal cruelty, marriage equality, politics, the environment, health concerns. Special interest groups may concentrate on art, cooking, video games, reading, music. Even though most major subjects already has a Facebook group supporting it, if someone is imaginative enough to find a group that does not already exist, they can easily create a group. While there are many social groups on the site, joining groups that support your career path, goals, and being affiliated with groups that helpful people are a part of, is a great way to make worthwhile connections and expand your network. These groups that you become associated with will also act as support beams for your personal brand, lending supplementary strength to your overall agenda.

Celebrity fan page:

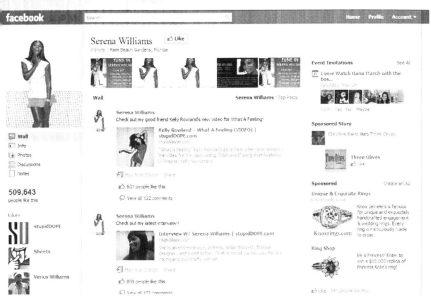

Similar to groups, users are able to create "**fan pages**," for a variety of reasons: athletes, teams, celebrities, events, movies, movements, and so on.

Not only is becoming a fan of a page a way to stay current with the happenings of a certain something, but creating a fan page is a great way to promote. Promote yourself. Promote your accomplishments. Promote your brand. Are you an aspiring artist who has piles of your paintings sitting in a corner waiting to show someone someday? Are you a guitar player with dreams of being "discovered" and folder filled of your homemade music videos gathering dust on your hard drive?

Create yourself a fan page. Post pictures of your artwork or videos of your songs and stop hiding your talents! Think of it as an electronic portfolio or as a fishing rod, with your talent as the bait. Flash it around to the right people, the "big fish," and make them bite! Creating a page that flaunts your talents and interests makes your brand an interactive entity, worthy of everyone's attention.

LinkedIn

Unlike the laid-back nature of Facebook, the focus of **LinkedIn** is much more professional. While Facebook began with, and likely continues to have, a focus on leisure and friendships, LinkedIn is a **business-oriented** social media site. Boasting over 100 million registered users worldwide (over half of which are in the United States), LinkedIn is the largest and most successful professional networking site. The main purpose of LinkedIn is to build a favorable connections between professionals, whether they be an employer, job seeker or employee, for business reasons such as job searching or company expansion.

Many of LinkedIn's features are reminiscent to those on Facebook; LinkedIn members create a profile, add a profile picture, include personal background information, join groups, send messages, and add "**connections**" rather than "friends." The difference, however, is the content of these features. Your LinkedIn profile will include the industry in which you work, your current company and job title, past companies and job titles, schools attended and degree obtained, and number of connections made. Below this brief list, you are able to explain exactly what you do at your job and give additional information about your company. This segment is followed by a more in-depth section about your education, including the schools you went to, the dates you were in attendance, your areas of study, degree(s) obtained, and any school organizations you were affiliated with.

I'm a student, not a working professional. Isn't it pointless to join LinkedIn?

No! Joining LinkedIn is a fantastic way to be proactive and lay the roundwork for your career in the future. Although the members of LinkedIn are predominately working professionals, the objective of the site is to allow members to connect with each other for career advice, growth and advancement. What better way is there for a student going to school for nursing to get career advice and line-up possible opportunities than by going on LinkedIn, making a connection with a nurse in the same area and initiating a conversation about how she started her career? While the opportunities listed on LinkedIn may not be immediately available to you as a student, immediate chances for internships, apprenticeship and mentorship may be available. Making connections and exploring their career paths, following companies and researching their professional objectives and joining groups and engaging in topical forums are great ways for a student member to take advantage of what LinkedIn has to offer.

What is especially unique about **LinkedIn** is the way you are able to go about gaining connections and expanding your network. In Facebook, your personal network consists of your friends and family. That's it. In LinkedIn, your personal network consists of your friends and family (direct connections), the connections of each of their connections (known as second-degree connections), and even the connections of your second-degree connections (known as third-degree connections). Your personal direct connections can then introduce you to other members that they are connected to, and...well...the chain just keeps growing.

This structure is especially helpful in situations where you are interested in a company, but do not know of anyone to contact. If you are interested in Company X and see that your teammate's mom is connected with the president of Company X on LinkedIn, you can request that she introduce you to him. People are able to write recommendations about their connections. Recommendations appear in the profile, and are extremely enticing to potential employers that may evaluate your profile, as they act as a **personal reference**.

LinkedIn direct 2nd and 3rd degree connections.

How you're connected to Mark

> **You**
> ⬇
> **Joe Black**
> **Joanne Walker**
> **Lindsay Jenkins**
> **Vincent Prince**
> **... and** 3 others
> ⬇
> (2nd) **Mark Smith**

In addition, judging by the information provided in your profile and the types of connections you already have in your network, **LinkedIn** will pull together a group of people with similar information and connections, and provide you with a list of people you may know. Basically, LinkedIn wants you to be connected with a world of people with interests similar to your own.

Because LinkedIn is a site focused on **professionalism and opportunities**, it has potential to work wonders for your personal brand. Throughout this book, you have been learning that personal branding is about putting your best foot forward, showing off your abilities and credentials and forging relationships to make the most of potential opportunities and reach your goals for success. LinkedIn is the perfect platform to market your brand in a professional way, and "sell yourself" to the people who matter.

Follow these tips to be sure that the power of LinkedIn is behind you and your brand.

1 Make sure your profile is detailed and complete.

2 Choose a clear, professional photo to add as your profile headshot.

3 Describe the responsibilities of your jobs in a way that highlights your abilities.

4 Include keywords and skills that apply to the field in which you want to be in.

5 Get and write recommendations. Having strong references strengthens your brand in the eyes of employers, and giving references shows that you care about the people you work with and that you understand what constitutes a strong employee.

6 If applicable, include links to your company and personal website, your blog or your online portfolio.

7 Build your network. Be constantly searching for connections that make sense to your network. The more connections you have, the more opportunities you have.

8 Make sure your profile is listed as "public" so members outside of your network are still able to view your general information.

9 Join and participate in groups relating to your professional industry. Follow companies in which you have an interest so you are easily able to see when they post new jobs or events.

TWITTER

While Facebook and LinkedIn are fairly intricate, **Twitter** is just the opposite. Twitter is described as a microblogging service, allowing its members to send and read short, 140-character messages known as **tweets.** The mood of Twitter is much more **laid back** and fun than other social media sites, and much, but not all, of its content is recreational. Twitter has gained massive popularity over the last two years, as can be seen in the sheer volume of users; the site has approximately 200 million users and harbors more than 65 million tweets a day.

Twitter is essentially an abbreviated version of the first two social media outlets. Rather than a detailed personal profile with photos and background information, a Twitter account consists only of a username (consisting by the "@" sign followed by a name- ex. @janedoe), picture, full name, location, personal website (if applicable), and one sentence long bio section. People in your Twitter network are deemed your "followers," or those you "follow." When you send a tweet, your followers will be able to see it; when the people you follow send a tweet, you will be able to see it. These tweets pop up to-the-second in your Twitter feed, which is on your homepage. If tweeting and texting were people, they would be cousins. Tweeting is commonly refered to as texting for the internet.

There are many ways to send, receive and share information, and each action is boiled down to a symbol.

It's a fun network to be a part of, so now is your chance to show your personality! The key to having Twitter success is to make your tweets are interesting enough to keep the attention of your followers, and grab the attention of potential people to follow you.

Because space is limited, it is important to get your point across in...well, 140-characters or less. Celebrities and athletes have seen a ton of Twitter success. Because tweeting is so quick and easy, it is an extremely effective way for those in the spotlight to communicate with their fans, updating them on daily activities, commenting on a TV show they are watching or asking a question to garner interaction with their followers. Because of this, Twitter is an easy, effective way of both promoting your personal brand to your network, and strengthening it through frequent interaction.

BE A BLOGGER

If you have a habit of speaking your mind, have strong opinions regarding any specific topic, have an extreme interest in an extracurricular activity, or just like to talk about your daily life happenings, starting a blog might be a good fit for you.

Blogging gives you the creative authority to write about whatever you desire to, and also makes your content available to the entire online network. Blogs are powerful self-promotion platforms, which is exactly what you are looking for when trying to build your personal brand.

Why you should Blog?

- It's **simple**, **easy** and **free**.
- Gives you access to a large group of people with your same interests.
- Allows you to be yourself under your own brand.
- Increases your **network** worth over social media platforms.
- The more you blog, the more **search results** with your name will appear.
- Establishing a blog gives you opportunities to network with other bloggers with complimenting interests.

Using Blogging to Build Your Brand

- It gives the perception you are an "expert" on your focus area, especially doing it for a prolonged period of time.
- Allows you to work on your writing skills to clearly define and explain what your brand represents.
- Attracting a group of people that can relate to your brand.

YOUTUBE & FLICKR

As **social media** evolves and expands, new media types are being integrated. While users are able to post videos and pictures to some social media sites, **YouTube** and **Flickr** are entities that focus solely on these personal pieces. Would you rather have someone tell you about the fireworks they saw on the 4th of July, or watch pictures and see an actual video of them?

Videos stimulate multiple senses and tell a complete story to the viewer. Photos are able to be saved and referred to over and over. These two sites are helpful in building your personal brand, as they give your audience a mental picture of you to coincide with the story they have read or heard. Branding is about balance. Incorporating visually stimulating social media sites into your online brand presence provides a comfortable balance to the written text of the other sites that you will use for your self-promotion.

Tips for using YouTube/Flicker

- Do not record/upload for more than **5 minutes** Keep it simple.

- Do add the links to other Social Media pages. Never lose sight of a chance for **self promotion**!

- **Comment** on other people's videos. It will help promote interaction with yours.

- Create video/picture series on topics relating to your brand.

- Run **contests** for your network.

- Keep in mind that the rules for appropriate content still apply.

Wrap Up:

- Social Media has both positive and negatives. Know the differences between the two and apply them to your personal branding plan.

- The best person to push you as a brand is none other than yourself. Use Social Media as a sounding board to reach your target audience and maintain relationships with current ones.

- Consistency can make or break your brand credibility. Make sure that your offline and online branding efforts and actions are cohesive.

- Make it a habit of searching your name online, and review what comes up. If something rings an alarm, make efforts to remove it immediately.

- Use Social Media as a way to search for information prior to interviewing or an important meeting. This gives you information to discuss on topics and interests that relate to everyone involved.

Create a short and to the point social media plan for your personal brand.

Answer the following questions as a start...

Exercises:

- What are my goals for using this type of medium? (i.e. Linkedin vs facebook)

_____
_____
_____

- What would my target audience be interested in hearing from me?

_____
_____
_____

- How often do I have to make a lasting impression on my profile page?

_____
_____
_____

- How can I relate to my target audience so that they are interested in what I have to say?

_____
_____
_____

- Determine what your definition of success is before moving forward with executing your plan.

_____
_____
_____

- After you created a bases for your plan. Test it and evaluate your progress once a month. Tweak and try new tactics as you continue on your personal brand building. Use this chapter as a basis.

_____
_____
_____

Let us test your knowledge of Social Media. People once thought Social Media would be just a fad. Now it's part of our daily lives. Let us see how well you score on the following trivia!

"SOCIAL MEDIA ISN'T A FAD, IT'S A FUNDAMENTAL SHIFT IN THE WAY WE COMMUNICATE"
- ERIK QUALMAN

TRUE OR FALSE?

1. _____ 50% of the world's population is under 30 years old. 96% of them have joined a social network.
2. _____ Facebook tops Google for weekly traffic in the United States.
3. _____ Social Media is the #1 activity on the internet.
4. _____ U.S. Department of Education study revealed that online students out performed those receiving face to face instruction.
5. _____ 80% of companies use Social Media for recruitment. 95% of them use LinkedIn.

BONUS! (CIRCLE THE CORRECT ANSWER)

If Facebook were a country it would be the world's (**3rd, 4th, 6th or 12th**) largest.

PASS OR FAIL? Did you get all 5 correct? See the Answer Key at the back.

"WORD OF MOUTH HAS NOW BECOME WORLD OF MOUTH"

They're just like you.
No, really they are...

When most people think of a celebrity, they often remove themselves from being within that class system of people. You might often ask yourself "why not me" while wishing to be in that position. I am here to let you know that it is not as difficult as it may seem. It is very possible to be your **own** celebrity. With your **own** fan base. In your **own** market. Making your **own** history. Get it?... Great!

You may not have thousands of screaming fans and paparazzi standing outside your door for photo-ops but it is totally possible to use the same tools that celebrities do with their management and PR teams to create a world for your niche. While most successful people and celebrities have similarities in hard work, talent and perseverance at one point they had to decide on their brand identity. Let us start thinking about some of theirs and how it relates to your own.

As you review the next few pages, please keep this in mind. The goal of the following exercises is to strip away the idea that success is beyond your reach. Quite the opposite, it is within your grasps and simply up to you to take it. Use the successes and failures of others as an example for creating your own personal blueprint. Start viewing and seeing yourself as THE BEST. Consistently deliver it. Own it. As you implement the tools you have learned, keep in mind that in creating a new version of yourself does not mean becoming another person. Use these skills to fine tune yourself versus changing yourself.

So you have made it to the end. You can officially knight yourself as a B.ME personal branding graduate. Now, the real fun begins!

Let us apply the concepts and theories that you have learned throughout this book to some popular personal brands. As you review these case studies, think back on some of the things you have learned and how well did these personal brands measure on:

- Defining their personal brands.

- Surpassing their base industry to enter into other opportunities.

- Perception vs. reality.

- Implementation of applying differentiation.

- Involvement in community.

- Creating a genuine platform based on their background, personality, interests and life style.

- Effectiveness on communicating their platforms.

- Success at self-promotion.

- Image and appearance.

- Usage of social media.

> "I think it was the exposure of Michael Jordan; the marketing of Michael Jordan. Everything was marketed towards the things that people wanted to see."
>
> **–Michael Jordan**

Background

Simply known at the "Greatest Basketball Player of All Time" and arguably by many as the greatest athlete of all time, the name Michael Jordan rings bells as one of the most strongest and powerful personal brands. Jordan treats himself as a true business. If there were awards for iconic personal brand building, we quite possibly would have our winner! Becoming a household name, was not an easy fete but its base never changed- basketball. As Jordan proved himself on the court and within his profession, dubbing himself with many accolades as a renowned athlete, he propelled interest and built a fan base. He kept his focus and drive on being the best within his field. His personal brand's foundation led the way to having longevity and staying power.

Brand Traits-Characteristics-Attributes

Accomplished Basketball Player, Charismatic, Athletically Gifted, Team Leader, Intensely Competitive, Extremely Hard Working, Spokesperson, Champion

Brand Perception

By proving himself daily on the court and honing in on his gifts, Michael Jordan solidified his net worth as an untouchable athlete; one that is authentic and undeniable.

Path to Success

1. Michael tried out for the basketball team his sophomore year in high school and did not make the cut due to his height- 5'11"- which was considered short. Using that as motivation, he became the star of the junior varsity team. Continuing to build on his talent, he was named a McDonalds All-American his senior year averaging a triple double. While attending the University of North Carolina at Chapel Hill, Jordan perfected his skill to another level. He racked in several awards and honors, including hitting the game winning shot in the NCAA 1982 Championship.

2. As a professional athlete with the Chicago Bulls, Jordan continued to shatter records on the court, which parlayed into a special opportunity for his Nike deal. His success as basketball's "airness" translated to phenomenal sales for what we affectively know now simply as Jordans. Endorsement deals with other prominent brands were secured and to this day currently exist.

3. Jordan's legacy does not only include basketball records and endorsement dollars. He has left his mark and still continues to with charitable organizations by donating millions to several children charities.

4. As a retired player, Jordan continues to use his brand by being a part of Brand Jordan and by building on the co-branding relationships he created while being a professional athlete. Never leaving far from his base, he is currently the majority owner and head of basketball operations for the NBA's Charlotte Bobcats.

Reflection

• Compare Michael Jordan's attributes to your own. What would close family and friends say about you? Compare them to how you view yourself and what you would like to be viewed as by your peers and influential circle.

_____
_____
_____
_____
_____
_____
_____
_____
_____
_____
_____

• Jordan's commonality of his brand building remains basketball. He found creative ways to stay tied in with the culture but build out from that community for his own brand. What is your foundation for your brand? It should be something that you are passionate about and you feel compelled to pursue. The road to personal branding is not a short one. Choose wisely.

_____
_____
_____
_____
_____
_____
_____
_____
_____
_____

Michael Jordan

On a scale from 1-5, with 5 being the greatest and 1 being the least; from your personal perspective, how well did **Michael Jordan** perform on the following:

Defining His Personal Brand
1   2   3   4   5

Surpassing His Base Industry to Enter New Opportunities
1   2   3   4   5

Perception vs Reality
1   2   3   4   5

Implementation and Applying Differentiation
1   2   3   4   5

Community Involvement
1   2   3   4   5

Genuine Platform Based on Background, Personality, Interest, and Lifestyle
1   2   3   4   5

Communication Effectiveness
1   2   3   4   5

Self-Promotion Success
1   2   3   4   5

Image and Appearance
1   2   3   4   5

Social Media Usage
1   2   3   4   5

"I haven't tried to go out of my way to inspire people. When you're real and you're authentic and you try to give honest answers all the time, then it's easy."

–Danica Patrick

Background

Mention the name Danica Patrick and many words should come to mind, at the forefront being- pioneer. While Danica is not the first woman to hold the title of professional racecar driver, she certainly has made waves in the sport like no other woman to date. Causing quite a stir has been Danica's specialty while driving interest and chatter about her personal brand in the sport. She has used her envelope pushing commercials to build a brand around herself. While her male counterparts traditionally used their attributes and personality to make a buzz, she's done the same while relying on her femininity to market herself in addition to her driving ability. Breaking records and barriers have become Danica's area of expertise in the business of car racing and mass marketing. While much talk about Danica focuses on her individually, she is a fierce competitor, securing titles in Rookie of the Year for both the IndyCar series and the Indianapolis 500.

Brand Traits-Characteristics-Attributes

Accomplished Athlete, Self-Motivated, Extremely Hard Working, Spokesperson, Determined, Fearless

Brand Perception

Danica Patrick commands attention by being an excellent athlete and being in charge of her image for success in her career.

Path to Success

1. Originally from Wisconsin, Danica started racing go-karts at 10 years old. She showed so much talent at a young age that she moved to England at 16 to compete in the prestigious Formula Ford series. She earned a second-place in Britain's Formula Ford Festival, the highest finish by a woman in the event.

2. Danica Patrick continued breaking records as her professional career moved over to IndyCar. In her debut in the Indianapolis 500, she became the first woman to lead the famed race and roared to a fourth-place finish at more than 220 mph.

3. Despite her landmark placing, Danica struggled, like many racers do in securing sponsorship deals and marketing opportunities. In a risky decision that panned out for her to this date, she changed racing teams, management and found a new sponsor in GoDaddy. With that change, much followed suit with a building fanbase due to new marketing tactics based around her femine appeal.

4. As with many successes, there are down moments. CBS banned one of her three commercials for Super Bowl XLV because it was too outrageous to air.

5. Danica became the first woman to lead a lap at Daytona International Speedway in the NASCAR Nationwide Series. While there is much to say about her off-track marketing tactics, she has the talent to back up her tenacity.

Reflection

• Being a woman in a male dominated sport usually comes with a lot of challenges that you are expected to face daily. Danica's love and enthusiasm for car racing seems to trump all the negativity that comes her way. She has many competitors that wish her well and respect her and others who do not. If you are a female, what special attributes about your brand do you feel is helpful in similar situations. If you are a male, what special attributes in your brand do you feel help deal with communicating with the opposite sex in a work setting?

_____
_____
_____
_____
_____
_____
_____

• Danica has used out of the box measures in using her image to market herself. While it came with much overall success, she has to deal with critics and often is put in a position to stand up for herself. In building your brand, there are times where you may feel strongly about something that others do not. How do you plan on handling negative feedback?

_____
_____
_____
_____
_____
_____

Danica Patrick

On a scale from 1-5, with 5 being the greatest and 1 being the least; from your personal perspective, how well did **Danica Patrick** perform on the following:

Defining Her Personal Brand
1   2   3   4   5

Surpassing Her Base Industry to Enter New Opportunities
1   2   3   4   5

Perception vs Reality
1   2   3   4   5

Implementation and Applying Differentiation
1   2   3   4   5

Community Involvement
1   2   3   4   5

Genuine Platform Based on Background, Personality, Interest, and Lifestyle
1   2   3   4   5

Communication Effectiveness
1   2   3   4   5

Self-Promotion Success
1   2   3   4   5

Image and Appearance
1   2   3   4   5

Social Media Usage
1   2   3   4   5

113

"Never Say Never"
— **Justin Bieber**

Background

After posting dozen of videos to YouTube, and having over 10 million views just from word of mouth, there had to be something special about his talent. Thanks to social media, Justin Bieber's talent was recognized and skyrocketed his career. Mistakenly, marketing director of SoSo Def, Scooter Braun had clicked on the wrong YouTube video coming across Justin's video. Never quite knowing when an opportunity would surface, Justin was ready, not just lucky. Scooter Braun was impressed and tracked him down. Suddenly, he was flying to Atlanta, Georgia for recording tracks, and a week later Justin had the opportunity to sing for the R&B pop star Usher. It was not an easy win with getting Usher's attention but after constantly pursuing him, Justin was signed, and just like that, another dream came true.

Brand Traits-Characteristics-Attributes

Carefree, Relevant-Now, Talented, Handsome, Appealing, Charming, Naturally Artistic, Ambitious

Brand Perception

Justin Bieber is social media's prince with traction to one day become King.

Path to Success

1. Justin Bieber grew up below the poverty line, where his mother survived off of church hand-outs to take care of the family. Using his talent as a distraction and dreams of making it big, Justin started singing and posting videos on YouTube for his family and friends who could not attend his performances.

2. After being scouted out by SoSo Def's marketing Manager Scooter Braun, Justin was signed by artist Usher Raymond to his label. It took several meetings and persistence on Justin's part to ensure his opportunity with Usher.

3. Making the transition to America, moving from his home in Canada took a bit of time for him to get accustomed to. Not allowing anything to get the best of him, he used his dream of making it, as his drive to press onward.

4. Bieber's debut of his first single "One Time " was released, and from then on Justin's career sky rocketed and so did his fan-base. There were not many competing artists within his age group, which solidified him taking advantage of an opportunity once it presented itself. He has broken records with his first movie, "Never Say Never" documenting his life and road to success.

"If you don't dream big, there's no use of dreaming. If you don't have faith, there's nothing worth believing."
–Justin Bieber

Reflection

• Justin has secured his fan base to ensure that he excels as he gets older. He did this by captivating his audience early enough to have them grow with him. How do you plan on having your audience grow with you for the life of your brand?

_____
_____
_____
_____
_____
_____
_____

• Justin took advantage of opportunities as they arouse in his life. He started posting videos online simply for his friends and family and they took on a life of their own. If he was not prepared vocally and able to show his talent to the music representatives he crossed paths with, he might have let his career opportunity slip by. What talents and skills do you have, that if you constantly worked on it, may open opportunities for you?

_____
_____
_____
_____
_____
_____
_____

Popular Personal Brands Grading Sheet

Justin Beiber

On a scale from 1-5, with 5 being the greatest and 1 being the least; from your personal perspective, how well did **Justin Beiber** perform on the following:

Defining His Personal Brand
1 2 3 4 5

Surpassing His Base Industry to Enter New Opportunities
1 2 3 4 5

Perception vs Reality
1 2 3 4 5

Implementation and Applying Differentiation
1 2 3 4 5

Community Involvement
1 2 3 4 5

Genuine Platform Based on Background, Personality, Interest, and Lifestyle
1 2 3 4 5

Communication Effectiveness
1 2 3 4 5

Self-Promotion Success
1 2 3 4 5

Image and Appearance
1 2 3 4 5

Social Media Usage
1 2 3 4 5

"In my mind, I'm always the best. If you walk out on the court and you think the next person is better, you've already lost."
-Venus Williams

"Nothing comes to a sleeper but a dream. Our Dad used to say that. It's an adage."
–Serena Williams

Background

Consistently ranked on top lists, The Williams sisters have amazed the world with their undeniable talents. The sporty siblings acknowledge their talent in the sport and used it as a tool to propel themselves to success. Venus and Serena began competing before they were five years old, entering their first tennis tournament at four and a half years old. Due to the vision their father Richard Williams had of both of his daughters being tennis champions, it encouraged them to live his dream. Throughout the years of growing up in Compton, California, where there is excessive gang activity it was tough for the two sisters to focus. They excelled by blocking out all the violence surrounding them and focusing solely on their dreams. With their signature style and play, Venus and Serena changed the look of the sport. They make themselves stand out as two individual public figures while still being a part of a unit. Though they are at times put in group situations, they still distinguish their individuality by being themselves.

Brand Traits-Characteristics-Attributes

Talented, Athletic, Driven, Consistent, Outgoing, Unique Fashion Sense, Down- to- Earth, Family Oriented, Religious

Brand Perception

Venus and Serena Williams are the most famous and competitive siblings in the world of sports.

Path to Success

1. Venus and Serena were taught to defend themselves with their rackets since infancy, being trained by their father at the tough tennis courts in Compton. Venus became a professional tennis player at the age of 14. At the age of 13, Serena attended her first professional event in Quebec City and lost the very first round.

2. The sisters early success started between the years of 1997-99 traveling all over the world playing athletes who were considered the best until Venus and Serena came along. Overcoming a few losses and injuries during their tennis tournaments, it never stop them from coming back to win the champion title.

3. Venus pulled out all the stops in 2006 when she published a letter directed to Wimbledon for not awarding equal prize money for both male and female tennis athletes. An overwhelming response was received and she was accredited to a significant change in history because of her willingness to speak up on behalf of the sport.

4. The sisters continue blazing new trails as they are the first African-American females to have ownership in an NFL team becoming new part-owners in the Miami Dolphins.

Reflection

• Venus and Serena used their determination to succeed to be able to surpass their community circumstances. They looked far and beyond what was given to them as a means of living to create something for themselves. Is there a circumstance in your life that makes you feel it holds you back from achieving your dreams? How can you use your will to succeed to break through it?

_____
_____
_____
_____
_____
_____
_____

• Although Venus and Serena are very close, they have been able to manage being their own selves and not stand in the other's shadow. How can you use the same principles they did by being a part of a group but letting your individuality show?

_____
_____
_____
_____
_____
_____

Venus & Serena Williams

On a scale from 1-5, with 5 being the greatest and 1 being the least; from your personal perspective, how well did **Venus** and **Serena** perform on the following:

Defining Their Personal Brand
1 2 3 4 5

Surpassing Their Base Industry to Enter New Opportunities
1 2 3 4 5

Perception vs Reality
1 2 3 4 5

Implementation and Applying Differentiation
1 2 3 4 5

Community Involvement
1 2 3 4 5

Genuine Platform Based on Background, Personality, Interest, and Lifestyle
1 2 3 4 5

Communication Effectiveness
1 2 3 4 5

Self-Promotion Success
1 2 3 4 5

Image and Appearance
1 2 3 4 5

Social Media Usage
1 2 3 4 5

"Don't let failure go to your heart,
and don't let success get to your head"
—Will Smith

Background

West Philadelphia born and raised,
Will Smith began rapping, and developing
his own slick, and semi-comic style with the influences
of Grandmaster Flash and Eddie Murphy. Will grew up
in a neighborhood where there was a melting pot of
cultures. Half of the population was Jewish and
Islamic. Yet, he still was adored by everyone for his
natural charm, silly pranks, which gave him the
nickname Prince. At 16, Will met the man who helped
him score his first world wide of success in the most
spontaneous way by firing fart spray into a fan at a
party impressing no one but Jazzy Jeff. The two
became a duo in the music industry, reaching
Billboard Charts and making countless hits. Will then
enhanced his name to the "Fresh Prince". There were
very risky decisions that Will chose by turning down
scholarships to high profile and prestigious universities
to pursue following his music career. His remarkable
crossover to acting came when he was able to be
the starring actor on NBC's sitcom Fresh Prince of
Bel-Air. That role marked the beginning of Will's acting
career, which has led him to starring in five star
movies, including the honor to star as the world's
greatest fighter Muhammad Ali. His first love of music
lead him to another opportunity of acting and a
crossover of being one of the Hollywood's most
bankable stars.

Brand Traits-Characteristics-Attributes

Intelligent, Talented, Funny, Inspiring Actor, Family
Oriented, Social Endeavor

Brand Perception

Will Smith holds the title of being the most successful
crossover star of our modern era.

Path to Success

1. Will started off as a rapper with his childhood friend Jazzy Jeff. Their speciality became humorous and radio friendly music. When it was time for Will to continue his education to pursue college, he turned down all scholarships to continue following his dreams. In a decision that worked in his favor, being young and early in his career Will freely spent his money and failed to pay his taxes which led him to financial bankruptcy.

2. Vowing to never make that mistake twice if he was given a second chance, he was back on track when he was offered the star role on *The Fresh Prince of Bel-Air*. From that point on Will's career furthered and excelled into Hollywood's movie industry, assisting him in reaching the goal of being "the world's biggest movie star".

3. The very same concepts he has applied and adhered to for himself, the same is said for his family, all of whom has similar success paths in the entertainment industry. Giving back to community is an integral part of his life. Many of his charitable affiliations include generous donations to children charities; including a school that both him and his wife have founded.

Reflection

• As a multi-talented performer, both as a rapper and an actor, Will had to make a decision on which one he would pursue, while putting the other on hold. It must not have been easy for him to stop making music while he focused on his acting career but he did. Do you have more than one talent that you are not sure what you should focus on? Make some reasons why you should focus on one over the other, or pursue both?

_____
_____
_____
_____
_____
_____
_____

• It is important to note that authenticity helped to create a core group of fans for Will's brand loyalty. Early in his career, his character played on *Fresh Prince of Bel-Air* essentially reflected himself. He was believable and relatable. He struck a chord with the audience because they believed him. How can you use your authenticity to ensure that you have a personal powerful brand?

_____
_____
_____
_____
_____
_____

Will Smith

On a scale from 1-5, with 5 being the greatest and 1 being the least; from your personal perspective, how well did **Will Smith** perform on the following:

Defining His Personal Brand
1 2 3 4 5

Surpassing His Base Industry to Enter New Opportunities
1 2 3 4 5

Perception vs Reality
1 2 3 4 5

Implementation and Applying Differentiation
1 2 3 4 5

Community Involvement
1 2 3 4 5

Genuine Platform Based on Background, Personality, Interest, and Lifestyle
1 2 3 4 5

Communication Effectiveness
1 2 3 4 5

Self-Promotion Success
1 2 3 4 5

Image and Appearance
1 2 3 4 5

Social Media Usage
1 2 3 4 5

"For me, it's about the way I carry myself and the way I treat other people."

-Beyoncé

Background

Beyoncé. The name, in and of itself, brings to mind images of glitz and glamour. You would be surely mistaken if you thought this notation was by accident. From Beyoncé's beginning years as being a part of her first girl group Girls Tyme to the now known Destiny's Child, being a solo star was always the goal from a carefully executed strategic plan. Destiny's Child, was a force to be reckoned with as Beyoncé became one of the biggest stars in the world that we know to date. The creation of what we now refer to simply as Beyoncé, didn't arrive to destination success on her own. Her seal-proof management team have put in major time and effort in crafting both her image and fine tuning the vocal trademark that she uses today. While there are many singers with great vocal ability, not many appear to have the entire package the way she does. Even while dressed in full glamour, she has a natural openness for being the girl next door. She found a way to blend her feminine appeal with a modest disposition. This exciting mix has solidified her as a star.

Brand Traits-Characteristics-Attributes

Accomplished, Innovative, Self-Disciplined, Entrepreneur, Self-Motivated, Giving, Strong-Minded, Resilient, Beautiful, Relatable

Brand Perception

Beyoncé is a poised, mastery of perfection.

Path to Success

1. Beyoncé's road to success began way before we knew she existed. Her talent and passion for performing, both singing and dancing, were noted as early as 5 years old. Her first group called Girl Tyme attracted a lot of attention in Houston, Texas almost immediately.

2. Gruesome and intense training hours averaging six hours a day paid off as they were given the opportunity to perform on Star Search. They lost in the finals of the show and suffered a major blow to what they thought would be their chance to make it "big".

3. With a management change of adding Beyoncé's father, Matthew Knowles, member replacements and an official name change to *Destiny's Child*, a new plan was put in to place to make the group world-wide stars. Dancing lessons, after singing lessons, after rehearsal lessons, summed up the larger part of their days.

4. Destiny's Child went on to be one of the most successful girl groups of all time.

5. While leaving the group to become a solo artist, although it was difficult, Beyoncé understood it was the next phase in her journey. With her debut release of Dangerously In Love, she won five Grammy awards. Several additional awards and numerous accolades followed suit in endorsement deals and movie appearances.

6. Her hard work and dedication to achieving her dream has shown through many of her achievements. Juggling several titles, being a singer, producer, songwriter, dancer, actress, and fashion designer, it would appear that things would slow down for her. Just quite the opposite, all facets have yet to peak and continue on an upward motion for more success that is yet to be written.

Reflection

• One of the things that has helped Beyoncé in terms of branding is that she is relatable to her audience. Co-branding is a large part of her success. The brands that she chooses to partner with always send messages that her audience can actually believe in. There is a reason why her products sell. She makes you believe that Pepsi will really quench your thirst. Her campaigns with L'Oreal verify your feeling of being "worth it". What are some other brands that you would like to work with that are comparable to your own? Focus on brands within your area that you could network and use a platform for your talents.

_____
_____
_____
_____
_____
_____
_____

• Beyoncé worked to become a brand, not just a performer. Her hard work has certainly paid off now that she can reap the fruits of her labor. A vision and greater plan was thought out. What's your "big picture"? Make it something you think is impossible to achieve. Then complete it.

_____
_____
_____
_____
_____
_____
_____

Beyoncé

On a scale from 1-5, with 5 being the greatest and 1 being the least; from your personal perspective, how well did **Beyonce** perform on the following:

Defining Her Personal Brand
1   2   3   4   5

Surpassing Her Base Industry to Enter New Opportunities
1   2   3   4   5

Perception vs Reality
1   2   3   4   5

Implementation and Applying Differentiation
1   2   3   4   5

Community Involvement
1   2   3   4   5

Genuine Platform Based on Background, Personality, Interest, and Lifestyle
1   2   3   4   5

Communication Effectiveness
1   2   3   4   5

Self-Promotion Success
1   2   3   4   5

Image and Appearance
1   2   3   4   5

Social Media Usage
1   2   3   4   5

"In my experience, there's only one thing that will always steer you toward success: That's to have a vision and to stick with it... Once I have a vision for a new venture, I'm going to ride that vision until the wheels come off."

-Russell Simmons

Background

Russell Simmons is akin to that of a culture defining pioneer. At the cutting edge of hip-hop's formation, he created Def Jam records and later fused that culture into clothing company, Phat Farm. Often grouped with lists of Most Influential People, his personal brand building continues to soar. He has found the pathway of his myriad avenues creating his personal brand. Consistently gives back to the community is a recurring theme with him. His philosophy with giving back stays consistent with all he does. Simmons is a mentor to other music icons including Sean "Diddy" Combs and Shawn "Jay-Z" Carter. Coining the phrase 'Do You' he is known to many for always being able to execute anything he values and wants to do.

Brand Traits-Characteristics-Attributes

Strong Sense of Purpose, Self Belief, Passionate, Spiritual, Compassionate, Embraces Change as Ppportunities, Perfectionist, Immaculate Work Ethic

Brand Perception

Russell Simmons is the relatable teacher that we can all relate to. His encouraging words and realness make us believe.

Path to Success

1. Russell Simmons co-founded one of hip-hops first record labels Def-Jam Records and managed the pioneering group Run DMC to success.

2. As his music efforts began to soar, he saw an opening in the world of fashion. Simmons struggled with his clothing line for two years trying to make it successful . Friends and business associates would laugh at him but his belief in himself triumphed once Phat Farm began to take off.

3. As Russell got older, he never steered away from the base of people who he attributes to as his audience. His philanthropic work with hip-hop summits, writing books, and other charitable causes have been consistent on getting insight on how to become successful in life.

> **"Whatever obstacles appear in your path, put your head down and get past them. Those obstacles aren't real. They're just God's way of testing you. He's asking you, Do you want to make it or not? "**
> **-Russell Simmons excerpt from 'Do You'**

Reflection

• Russell Simmons' brand message was clearly defined since the start of Def-Jam Records. He stayed true to himself through years of brand building. Simmons has conquered over many different obstacles but kept his family, faith and religion first. What is your personal message and how do you plan on incorporating it in everything that you do?

_____

_____

_____

_____

_____

_____

_____

• Giving back to your community helps your image not only by the kind act itself but strengthens your relationship with your audience. What will you do to help your community grow? How can you help people build their self-confidence and help them towards their dreams in life?

_____

_____

_____

_____

_____

_____

Russell Simmons

On a scale from 1-5, with 5 being the greatest and 1 being the least; from your personal perspective, how well did **Russell Simmons** perform on the following:

Defining His Personal Brand
1 2 3 4 5

Surpassing His Base Industry to Enter New Opportunities
1 2 3 4 5

Perception vs Reality
1 2 3 4 5

Implementation and Applying Differentiation
1 2 3 4 5

Community Involvement
1 2 3 4 5

Genuine Platform Based on Background, Personality, Interest, and Lifestyle
1 2 3 4 5

Communication Effectiveness
1 2 3 4 5

Self-Promotion Success
1 2 3 4 5

Image and Appearance
1 2 3 4 5

Social Media Usage
1 2 3 4 5

Case Studies: Taylor Swift
Country Pop Queen

"Being FEARLESS isn't being 100% Not FEARFUL, it's being terrified but you jump anyway..."
    -Taylor Swift

Background

Coming from Wyomissing, Pennsylvania, where there are not many activities for a teenage girl, music became Taylor Swift's release of her emotions. After being seen as a misfit in school, she would write poetry and novels. Writing her own songs was used as a way to express herself. She began performing locally at festivals and joining karaoke contests as well. Taylor began taking trips to Nashville, Tennessee to work with local song writers, and gave her demo tape to every label in town. After being rejected by all the labels, given the opportunity of a lifetime, Taylor was invited to the U.S. Open tennis tournament to sing the National Anthem. She blew the crowd away and eventually was picked up at a songwriter's festival. By keeping her brand on her own terms, she was able to be the type of artist she envisioned, both for herself and her audience. Believing in herself, she backed out of contracts that did not allow her to sing or write her own songs at the age of 14. She is now country's music reigning sweetheart.

Brand Traits-Characteristics-Attributes

Beautiful, Down to Earth, Outgoing, Creative, Independent, Pop Star, Avid Storyteller

Brand Perception

Taylor Swift is the modern all American girl.

Path to Success

1. By the age of 10, Taylor was performing locally, and began writing songs at the age of 12. As she felt more comfortable being a performer, she reached out to local songwriters in Nashville, Tennessee.

2. She later entered in a Nashville songwriters contest, and caught the eye of Scott Borchetta who signed her to his newly formed record label, Big Machine Records. She was then one of the youngest staff writers at the label.

3. In 2006, Taylor debut single *Tim McGraw* reached the billboard music chart as one of the hottest country songs.

4. Today, Taylor Swift is one of the most popular artists and songwriters in mainstream music. She has been described as one of pop's finest songwriters and given much acclaim for being more in touch with her inner life than most adults.

> **"To me, Fearless is not the absense of fear. It's not being completely unafraid. To me, Fearless is having fears. Fearless is having doubts. Lots of them. To me, Fearless is living in spite of those things that scare you to death."**
> **−Taylor Swift**

Reflection

• Taylor was turned away by several labels but she continued believing in herself that her chance would appear. How can you keep a fearless attitude and keep pushing on despite negative circumstances in your way?

_____
_____
_____
_____
_____
_____

• Taylor is known just as much for writing her own songs as she is for singing them. While most artists, choose to sing songs by writers other than themselves, she always uses her words from her own experiences which make it more believable and authentic for her fans. What are some things that you can do with your talent to make sure that you remain authentic for your audience?

_____
_____
_____
_____
_____
_____

Taylor Swift

On a scale from 1-5, with 5 being the greatest and 1 being the least; from your personal perspective, how well did **Taylor Swift** perform on the following:

Defining Her Personal Brand
1 2 3 4 5

Surpassing Her Base Industry to Enter New Opportunities
1 2 3 4 5

Perception vs Reality
1 2 3 4 5

Implementation and Applying Differentiation
1 2 3 4 5

Community Involvement
1 2 3 4 5

Genuine Platform Based on Background, Personality, Interest, and Lifestyle
1 2 3 4 5

Communication Effectiveness
1 2 3 4 5

Self-Promotion Success
1 2 3 4 5

Image and Appearance
1 2 3 4 5

Social Media Usage
1 2 3 4 5

Case Studies: Jennifer Lopez
Genie of Many Talents

"You get what you give. What you put into things is what you get out of them"
–Jennifer Lopez

Background

Remarkably one of the most influential women in entertainment history, Jennifer Lopez has independently become a household name. Altering from a precocious Catholic schoolgirl to an honorable businesswoman, exceptional actress, dancer and singer, and notable fashion designer, TV personality and producer; JLo has successfully rocked and diversified the entertainment world over the past decade. She has captivated many with her dazzling physical attributes, enduring mannerisms and admirable talents, all the while using her parents' work ethics as a basis for her success. The journey to becoming a powerful multi-millionaire was not always reassuring. Jennifer began as a devalued dancer in the Bronx sleeping in the studios and gyms where she practiced. She progressed her dancing skills, landing her jobs in various shows and music videos. She later became interested in acting, which led her to the controversial role of slain Latina singer Selena, in which Lopez magnificently fulfilled. Jennifer is a self-made success story. She proved no matter where you come from, or what you have gone through, turning dreams into reality is always a possibility if you just believe and followup with hard work.

Brand Traits-Characteristics-Attributes

Versatile Entertainer, Multi-talented, Goal Oriented, Motivated, Captivated Icon, Beloved Activist, Industrious Winner

Brand Perception

Jennifer Lopez has flourishingly utilized her many talents as an elevation platform.

Path to Success

1. After being turned down at the audition the first time, Jennifer Lopez caught her first big break as a dancer on the hit 90's sitcom *In Living Color*.

2. Playing the role of *Selena* launched Jennifer into what we now know as her multifaceted career. Furthering the buzz of her performance in the movie, her followup was her own musical debut album *On the 6*.

3. Always ambitious in merging all of talents together, much of what she does includes at least two of her skills in acting, singing, dancing or fashion.

4. After a brief hiatus to start a family, she returned to the lights being one of three hosts on American Idol, and releasing her 7th studio album *Love?* Never known for taking a break for too long, her career has been ignited for yet another run at success.

> **"I think crossroads come at many times during your life. Up to this point, I`ve had several. You get to a certain point in your life and you`re like, Am I supposed to be doing this? And it`s usually in the face of some failure - something that didn`t work out the way you wanted it to. And you`re faced with a decision: Do I keep trying to do this or do I give up?"**
> **–Jennifer Lopez**

Reflection

• Jennifer Lopez is very skilled at making all her talents prosper. Despite enduring many obstacles, rejections, and setbacks throughout her life, Lopez still managed to make her dreams become a reality with the help of determination and drive. Name two of your many talents and skills. How can you use them together to make sure that you're seen in a better light and also possibly open more doors and opportunities for you?

_____
_____
_____
_____
_____
_____
_____

• Being inviting with her personal life, has been a positive and negative, for Jennifer. It is important to have balance between what you share outwardly to people and what you keep private to yourself. What are some things that you plan to keep personal and private to yourself?

_____
_____
_____
_____
_____
_____

Jennifer Lopez

On a scale from 1-5, with 5 being the greatest and 1 being the least; from your personal perspective, how well did **Jennifer Lopez** perform on the following:

Defining Her Personal Brand
1 2 3 4 5

Surpassing Her Base Industry to Enter New Opportunities
1 2 3 4 5

Perception vs Reality
1 2 3 4 5

Implementation and Applying Differentiation
1 2 3 4 5

Community Involvement
1 2 3 4 5

Genuine Platform Based on Background, Personality, Interest, and Lifestyle
1 2 3 4 5

Communication Effectiveness
1 2 3 4 5

Self-Promotion Success
1 2 3 4 5

Image and Appearance
1 2 3 4 5

Social Media Usage
1 2 3 4 5

"Remind yourself. Nobody built like
you, you design yourself."
– Jay-Z

Background

He is not a businessman. He is a business, man! Jay-Z,
a shortened version of his childhood nickname- Jazzy,
holds many titles, all of which he has garnered much
success. Self described as "the black Warren Buffett",
he is a musician, media mogul and entrepreneur with
a worth estimated at least half a billion dollars. Jay-Z's
success has always been centered around a keen
ability he naturally has to understand and influence
his personal brand via many mediums. While there
are several hip-hop artists with powerful brands, non
have secured the corporate and mass-market with
street credibility as he has. Although the streets
"raised him", his personal goals pushed him and
continued to give him the drive to break many
stereotypes and set a path for future urban artists that
came after him. Where comparable counterparts
have failed, Jay-Z has done an impeccable job
understanding a fine balance with his marketability
and authenticity.

Brand Traits-Characteristics-Attributes

Accomplished Rap Artist, Hustler, Entrepreneur, Gifted,
Extremely Hard Working, Spokesperson, Talented,
Strong-Minded, Creative, Winning Attitude

Brand Perception

Jay-Z is an entertainment powerhouse and the most
powerful influence on hip-hop culture.

Path to Success

1. At an early age, Jay-Z found his love of music, playing it often and loudly, waking up those that surrounded the house. During that time, he honed in on a natural gift being able to create an entire song without writing it down once.

2. He took it upon himself to sell his own CDs out the trunk of his car. His first big break occurred when he landed a spot alongside Big Daddy Kane on a popular track at the time.

3. After getting turned away from larger labels and always known for keeping his eye on business deals, he started Roc-A-Fella records.

4. Striking while the iron was hot, he had several singles on the airwaves at once, making him a mainstay contender in the hip-hop world.

5. Taking note from other mentors, he started businesses that propelled him and was relative to the audience and fan base that helped him rise to success. Music labels, nightclubs, sports teams and clothing brands bear his influence and ownership of the Jay-Z lifestyle.

> **"I will not lose for even in defeat, there's a valuable lesson learned so it evens up for me."**
> **-Jay-Z**

Reflection

• Jay-Z's success surrounded much around him treating himself as a business, not just an artist. He made different decisions that set him apart from comparable artists. He opened up new lanes for himself that navigated new opportunities. What are some decisions you can make to help with opening new opportunities for you?

_____

_____

_____

_____

_____

_____

• It's no secret of Jay-Z's winning attitude. He rarely ever embarks on a new venture without planning to win it all. Failures are also apart of successes. He experienced failures in several projects but did not hamper on them, allowing it to never affect the perception of the brand of "Jay-Z". As you experience your failures, what will be your drive to persevere?

_____

_____

_____

_____

_____

_____

Jay Z

On a scale from 1-5, with 5 being the greatest and 1 being the least; from your personal perspective, how well did **Jay Z** perform on the following:

Defining His Personal Brand
1   2   3   4   5

Surpassing His Base Industry to Enter New Opportunities
1   2   3   4   5

Perception vs Reality
1   2   3   4   5

Implementation and Applying Differentiation
1   2   3   4   5

Community Involvement
1   2   3   4   5

Genuine Platform Based on Background, Personality, Interest, and Lifestyle
1   2   3   4   5

Communication Effectiveness
1   2   3   4   5

Self-Promotion Success
1   2   3   4   5

Image and Appearance
1   2   3   4   5

Social Media Usage
1   2   3   4   5

"I've never been surprised about what happened to me. I've put in hard work to get to this point"
—Sean John Combs

Background

From Puff Daddy to P. Diddy, mediocre party promoter to the richest figure in hip-hop, Sean John Combs has transcended into an astonishing hip-hop mogul, businessman, entertainer, record producer and fashion designer. Interning at Uptown Records proved essential in the establishment of his success in the entertainment and business world. There, he became a talent director, which led to the creation of his empire Bad Boy Records and his business involvement with numerous top-selling artists, including Usher, Lil Kim, TLC, Notorious B.I.G., Mary J. Blige, and Boyz to Men. Although his career seemed to be working in his favor, his illuminated reign in the entertainment industry was frequently eclipsed by criticism and various negative events, including many business disputes, several lawsuits and other legal troubles. Sean since then has turned his hardships into triumphs, by fueling his talents into rapping, acting, singing, designing clothes, and managing new artists. He has won Grammy awards, landed roles in highly credited movies such as Monster's Ball, and is involved in many business ventures. He continues to be a powerful influence to anyone with goals and dreams, and can be located in Forbes magazine as the richest Hip-Hop mogul to date.

Brand Traits-Characteristics-Attributes

Vigorous Worker, Persevering Entrepreneur, Comical Entertainer, Creative Flair, Survivor, Hit-Making Genius

Brand Perception

Sean John Combs is the King of hip-hop's reinvention.

Path to Success

1. During the early 90's, Sean interned at Uptown Records, traveling from New York and Washington, DC daily via the train. He later founded the now multi-million dollar Bad Boy Entertainment Record Company, which birthed countless successful artists.

2. His debut album *No Way Out* earned him a Grammy for best rap album. As his success continued to rise, trouble followed him. Turning negatives into a positive after settling several deathful suits from a stampede that happened at one of his concerts he started the re-imaging of himself by going through several name and image changes.

3. Utilizing the strength of his name, he created several projects including MTV's Making the Band, clothing lines, fragrances and opening his talents to acting. All of his projects reached much acclaimed success and continued adding value to his worth.

4. Being consistent with his new image, he gained major publicity as he trained to run the New York City Marathon, which he raised $2 million for the educational system in New York. Sean also was head of the "Vote or Die" campaign for the 2004 presidential election.

Reflection

• Sean wanted success so badly within music that he took it upon himself to take a train every day from New York to Washington DC for his internship. Some people may say that was extreme but it proved to himself and others just how bad he wanted to make it and achieve success. What are some things that you could do to achieve your goals that may be more along the lines of pushing the envelope, compared to others?

_____

_____

_____

_____

_____

_____

• Sean promotes himself daily, as his career moves it appears he does it even more so. No one works harder for himself than he does. Instead of waiting for others to make your dreams come true what can you do to self promote yourself?

_____

_____

_____

_____

_____

_____

Sean John Combs

On a scale from 1-5, with 5 being the greatest and 1 being the least; from your personal perspective, how well did **Sean John Combs** perform on the following:

Defining His Personal Brand
1 2 3 4 5

Surpassing His Base Industry to Enter New Opportunities
1 2 3 4 5

Perception vs Reality
1 2 3 4 5

Implementation and Applying Differentiation
1 2 3 4 5

Community Involvement
1 2 3 4 5

Genuine Platform Based on Background, Personality, Interest, and Lifestyle
1 2 3 4 5

Communication Effectiveness
1 2 3 4 5

Self-Promotion Success
1 2 3 4 5

Image and Appearance
1 2 3 4 5

Social Media Usage
1 2 3 4 5

"Do the one thing you think you cannot do. Fail at it. Try again. Do better the second time. The only people who never tumble are those who never mount the high wire. This is your moment. Own it."

-Oprah Winfrey

Background

Quite possibly the world's most powerful brand, Oprah Winfrey's story and attest to brand authenticity provides the best real life case study for personal branding. Oprah's genuine message of challenging people to live better lives was so craftily done that not many articles written about her fail to note that important point. The essence of Oprah is staying true to herself. She has built a fandom of millions simply because she is relatable. She is just like you. No different, and reiterated that daily in her talk shows. Consistency has been the glue that has held her base together and will continue to do so with time. She knows her audience intimately. After all, she attests to be one of them. A target audience of women, ages 25 to 54 has remained her foundation which has helped build generations of brand loyalty. It would be difficult to find a comparable brand where its audience puts as much trust in one person.

Brand Traits-Characteristics-Attributes

Strong Sense of Purpose, Self-Belief, Humble, Passionate, Spiritual, Compassionate, Embraces Change as Opportunities, Perfectionist, Immaculate Work Ethic, Public Vulnerability

Brand Perception

Oprah Winfrey is the American Dream that we all hope to aspire; she makes us believe in greater things.

Path to Success

1. Overcoming many hardships and poverty at a young age, Oprah started broadcasting at a local radio station. She worked her way up to local news, then hosted her own show. As her show's popularity increased and receivedsyndicated, she founded Harpo Studios (now Harpo, Inc.) to be her own boss and continue building the base of what we now know as "The Oprah Winfrey Empire".

2. Building on her personal successes, she held the title as an actress both in *The Color Purple* and *Beloved* while adding even more titles to her name.

3. The power of her influence, deems its own title, "The Oprah Effect". With a corporate controlling network of O magazine (circulation of more than 2 million), Book Club (largest in the world) , Oprah Radio, and knighting new stars like Dr. Phil and Rachel Ray, she signifies just how powerful her words and reach really can be. Her influence, stands alone, by increasing sales of anything she endorses.

4. As is the case with several successful public personal brands, Oprah does a fair share of giving back; with the Angel Network she has given over $80 million to charity. With her current personal network in OWN (Oprah Winfrey Network), the same philosophies she employed for her rise to success will certainly be used as a platform here.

Reflection

• Oprah's brand message was clearly defined since the start of her very first talk show. She stayed true to herself through years of brand building. What is your personal message? Has it been consistent so far?

_____

_____

_____

_____

_____

_____

_____

• In the weeks leading up to OWN's launch, you saw it everywhere. It was promoted so well (on television commercials, billboards, social media apps, etc.) that even if you were not an Oprah fan, you surely were aware that OWN existed. As you use social media to promote your own personal brand, how will you elevate yourself?

_____

_____

_____

_____

_____

_____

_____

Oprah

On a scale from 1-5, with 5 being the greatest and 1 being the least; from your personal perspective, how well did **Oprah** perform on the following:

Defining Her Personal Brand
1 2 3 4 5

Surpassing Her Base Industry to Enter New Opportunities
1 2 3 4 5

Perception vs Reality
1 2 3 4 5

Implementation and Applying Differentiation
1 2 3 4 5

Community Involvement
1 2 3 4 5

Genuine Platform Based on Background, Personality, Interest, and Lifestyle
1 2 3 4 5

Communication Effectiveness
1 2 3 4 5

Self-Promotion Success
1 2 3 4 5

Image and Appearance
1 2 3 4 5

Social Media Usage
1 2 3 4 5

Case Studies:
[WRITE YOUR NAME IN THE BOX]

[WRITE A QUOTE THAT YOU WOULD LIKE TO LIVE BY IN YOUR OWN WORDS.]

"

"

—
[YOUR NAME]

Background

[WRITE A SUMMARY OF YOUR STORY. IN THE LAST PARAGRAPH, FOCUS ON HOW YOU WOULD LIKE YOUR STORY TO BE WRITTEN FOR THE FUTURE.]

Brand Traits-Characteristics-Attributes

[LIST DESCRIPTIVE WORDS THAT GIVE INSIGHT TO WHO ARE.]

_____ , _____ ,
_____ , _____ ,
_____ , _____

Brand Perception

[PROVIDE A STRONG SENTENCE THAT HIGHLIGHTS HOW YOU WOULD LIKE YOUR BRAND TO BE VIEWED. REMEMBER WHAT YOU LEARNED WITH PERCEPTION VS REALITY.]

_____

_____

_____

_____

Case Studies:
[WRITE YOUR NAME IN THE BOX]

Path to Success

[HIGHLIGHT YOUR PATH TO SUCCESS, TO DATE, IN POINTS 1-2. IN POINTS 3-5 NOTE WHAT YOU WOULD LIKE YOUR JOURNEY TO LOOK LIKE AS YOU CONTINUE BUILDING YOUR BRAND.]

1.
_____
_____
_____
_____

2.
_____
_____
_____
_____

3.
_____
_____
_____

4.
_____
_____
_____

5.
_____
_____
_____

Reflection

• As you think back on the answers you noted about the previous personal brands, what can you tell overall about your own personal brand building?

_____
_____
_____
_____
_____
_____
_____
_____
_____
_____
_____
_____

• What popular personal brand do you most identify with? Why did you choose that person?

_____
_____
_____
_____
_____
_____
_____
_____
_____
_____
_____
_____
_____
_____

Your Personal Branding Grading Sheet

On a scale from 1-5, with 5 being the greatest and 1 being the least; how well did **YOU** perform on the following:

Defining your Personal Brand

1 2 3 4 5

Surpassing your Base Industry to Enter New Opportunities

1 2 3 4 5

Perception vs Reality

1 2 3 4 5

Implementation and Applying Differentiation

1 2 3 4 5

Community Involvement

1 2 3 4 5

Genuine Platform Based on Background, Personality, Interest, and Lifestyle

1 2 3 4 5

Communication Effectiveness

1 2 3 4 5

Self-Promotion Success

1 2 3 4 5

Image and Appearance

1 2 3 4 5

Social Media Usage

1 2 3 4 5

Want to Know More About B.ME?

The promotional possibilities of the information you learned in this book are endless. Amira Shiraz holds presentations, workshops and seminars, speaking to audiences both live and virtually. To keep up to date on the newest techniques, tools and information invite Amira to your next event or visit your online resource center at:

www.BrandingMyselfEveryday.com

It features free downloads and ongoing updated material from *B.ME! A Guide to Branding Myself Everyday*. If you would like one-on-one training, Amira offers online coaching programs both for groups and individuals.

Find out more online at www.AmiraShiraz.com.

Read It! Love it! Share it!

Book References and Suggested Further Reading

1. "*Expert Interview Body Language Tips.*" Job Interviews. Free Interview Questions and Answers and Job Interview Tips. 2010. Web. 20 Apr. 2011.
http://www.best-job-interview.com/interview-body-language.html

2. Garrett, Chris. "*How to Boost Your Personal Brand With Social Media | Social Media Examiner.*" Social Media Examiner: Your Guide to the Social Media Jungle. 21 Apr. 2010. Web. 28 Mar. 2011.
http://www.socialmediaexaminer.com/boost-personal-brand

3. Haefner, Rosemary. "*More Employers Screening Candidates via Social Networking Sites.*" Jobs - The Largest Job Search, Employment & Careers Site. 6 June 2009. Web. 4 Apr. 2011.
http://www.careerbuilder.com/Article/CB-1337-Interview-Tips-More-Employers-Screening-Candidates-via-Social-Networking-Sites

4. Montoya, Peter, and Tim Vandehey. *The Brand Called You: the Ultimate Brand-building and Business Development Handbook to Transform Anyone into an Indispensable Personal Brand.* [Santa Ana, Calif.]: Personal Branding, 2005. Print.

5. "*The Most Successful Advertising Slogans of All Time.*" Successful Advertising. 16 July 2010. Web. 3 Feb. 2011.
http://successfuladvertising.co.cc/successful-advertising-slogans-time.html

6. Rynge, Ola. "*Defining The Target Audience For Your Personal Brand | Brand-Yourself.com Blog.*" Personal Branding Brand-Yourself.com Blog. June 2010. Web. 15 Feb. 2011.
http://blog.brand-yourself.com/personal-brand/how-to-personal-brand/defining-the-target-audience-for-your-personal-brand

7. Schawbel, Dan. *Me 2.0: Build a Powerful Brand to Achieve Career Success.* New York: Kaplan Pub., 2009. Print.

8. Schawbel, Dan. "*Perception vs Reality in Social Media.*" Personal Branding Blog - Dan Schawbel. 25 Mar. 2010. Web. 19 Feb. 2011.
http://www.personalbrandingblog.com/perception-vs-reality-in-social-media

9. Martin, Gail. *30 Days to Social Media Success.* Career Press Pub., 2010. Print.

10. Qualman, Erik. Socialnomics: *How Social Media Transforms the Way We Live and Do Business.* Wiley, Pub., 2010. Print.

rngdnabi	branding
odgo	good
dba	bad
estioivp	positive
aeevigtn	negative
rnaoutipte	reputation
aieccicrsahsttr	characteristics
ane lmtmagei	mental image
zeaeogbnlcir	recognizable
leetablra	relatable
sisllk	skills
deai	idea
hm dnljoairaec	michael jordan
rhopa	oprah
yiaz	jayz
andnmao	madonna
oatnlumd dpr	donald trump
veelieb	believe
ieertcnopp	perception
ratyeil	reality
fesinlecnu	influences
eelards	leaders
flowreslo	followers
tseniicry	sincerity
ihittycatnue	authenticity
tinpertusopio	opportunities
rreeca	career

```
s e i a c l o n e s i a t o c n t
h l h d s t b a c k g r o u n d t
t s o g i t h i n e t a r o s o n
t r m r p e r s o n a l i t y e e
e c e n t h u s i a s t i c w t o
c n w e i n y y t s a a o t n d t
b y o i l c o u a c r m i c l t n
o f r i n y o c i t m s m o d t a
c b k e t l t n t u t l b m e e r
r h q i e a u s n s a o e f b n t
r d a y a m s i e e o c h o r d c
r s n r m o t r r f c b a r a c i
m n d o i y e i e o i t v t n d e
y d c n b t t i f v o l i z d e o
e u q i n u y r f m n g o o i e f
a o n i t r i d i e l o r n n t k
t a r g e t a u d i e n c e g t i
```

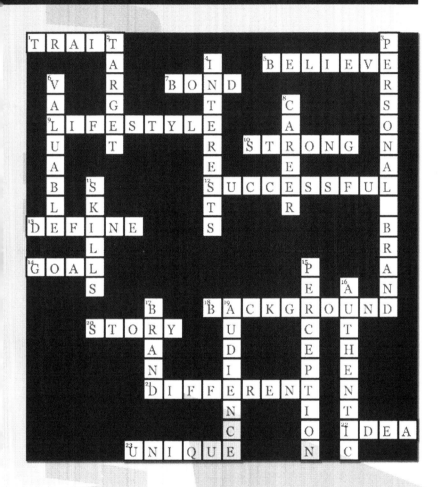

Communication is an essential part of ...

What people may perceive your brand as, is set by ...

Confidence in yourself helps people ...

Listening, taking your time, asking questions, using your body language and always being interested ...

A conversation during where information is gathered and conclusions are drawn amongst the participants ...

Researching and being informed prior to a meeting or interview ...

To increase your net worth for your branding communicating your brand is essential for ...

networking.

are tips for communicating effectively.

ensures you will be prepared for the conversation.

first impressions.

your Personal Brand.

believe in your brand.

qualifies as an interview.

163

1. Character 1, Character 3, Character 2

Character 1   **Character 3**   **Character 2**

2. Character 2, Character 3, Character 1

Character 2

Character 3

Character 1

TRUE OR FALSE?

1. **TRUE** 50% of the world's population is under 30 years old. 96% of them have joined a social network.

2. **TRUE** Facebook tops google for weekly traffic in the US

3. **TRUE** Social Media is the #1 activity on the internet

4. **TRUE** US Department of Education study revealed that online students out performed those receiving face to face instruction.

5. **TRUE** 80% of companies use Social Media for recruitment. 95% of them use LinkedIn.

CHOICES

If Facebook were a country it would be the world's **3rd** largest!

For comparison, look at the following chart of what the order of the top 5 countries would be:

1. CHINA
2. INDIA
3. FACEBOOK
4. UNITED STATES
5. BRAZIL

The Author

The Author

Amira Shiraz is the branding visionary and owner of Amira Shiraz, Inc. (ASI). A former model in the fashion industry, she is an entrepreneur and international speaker on personal branding and public awareness with a clientele that includes athletes, artists, small businesses, non-profits, and entertainment professionals both domestically and internationally.

A diverse background in writing, strategic planning, and traditional approaches to developing publicity and awareness allows her to transform the ordinary into the extraordinary with smooth execution, professionalism, and understanding of branding and how it relates to marketing and securing endorsements. Her experience lends itself to close to a decade in the marketing and branding fields of study.

Amira speaks to student audiences, on personal branding, self promotion and creating a path for success. Her one-on-one approach and enthusiasm for the subject matter lends itself well to personal sessions, workshops and seminars.

Amira lives in Philadelphia, Pennsylvania.
Contact Amira Shiraz at Amira@amirashiraz.com

ASI was established as a branding agency to assist talent that needed management for brand identity. They're the kind of agency that understands the importance of a personal brand, having worked with mainstream artists and athletes. Clients can be assured that their dedicated team will work tirelessly to ensure that their brand is always represented positively. Every client relationship begins with a comprehensive analysis of their brand which they use to develop a personalized branding strategy. ASI works tirelessly to develop valuable partnerships with organizations that champion their clients' causes and those that possess qualities they would like to be associated with. The agency started by catering specifically to the sports and entertainment industry but soon learned that personal branding for a more wider audience wasn't being accommodated to, and that has now become ASI's specialty.

The Program

At its inception, **B.ME!** started as a media training program , dedicated to athletes and entertainers at the beginning of their careers in teaching them how to build their brand identity. After receiving an overwhelming response, the program was broadened to that of a general personal branding program. It includes a three hour intensive workshop filled with audio visuals and reference content including a wrap up round table of someone who has exemplified tenure and excellence in their own personal branding. The instructors are certified of the knowledge and implementation of **B.ME!** Individuals, schools, sports teams, associations and organizations alike benefit from the workshop as an extension of the book to further grasp the concepts. As **B.ME!** continues to grow, we hope that you will continue to implement the tools and skills offered to you in our book and program for building your personal brand. The tactics offered in this book are expanded via our group workshops, personal seminars and home study programs.

Made in the USA
Lexington, KY
05 July 2012